Sindh and Balochistan

Sufism, Religions, and Ideologies

1

Zulfiqar Shah

AN ISM Publication

© Zulfiqar Shah 2019

CONTENTS

1

TRANSITION FOR INTERDEPENDENCE AND UNITY

Nations, continents, and their interrelations are the world body politic subsided by the culture. We need to have a leap beyond the faith in the world-order of these steady withering away contours. We have an international establishment in the form of United Nations; we were unable to transfer it into the world establishment. We have been attempting to translate the UN into virtual world establishment. This phase of ours is a bygone past. On the sidelines of UN reforms, we need to think as international community for a global order, to really transform ourselves for the climax of our new realities, challenges, and achievement. The concept and materialization of a world establishment of international community is yet un-conceived. We missed our own flight to our required destinations. Let us have a new rapid for the knock, which needs an open-up of a new door towards a global order and a real global establishment on the sidelines of globalization for our generations. This becomes unavoidable since world today is undergoing a phase in globalization in which national, ethnic and racial identity has started exhibiting itself. We have at least one lesson to be learned about, which is about the failed socialist states. Let us learn from the missing links of socialist states, which missed their leap from gradual socialism of state and society together due to structural socialism, and because of, statehood necessities.

Universality is the unity between and amongst the diversity. In the pedagogy, this phenomenon is called University. This includes interrelated nature of faculties, various disciplines of studies and research. This is an era of multi-disciplinary research in science, arts and humanity. The era of specialization is over now.

The philosophical history of Hegelian logic and dialectics as well as Marxian materialism until now has been misrepresented, inappropriately understood, and adopted by the majority. Let us think again, revisit the things briefly, and try to find nexus between apparently irrelevant factors. Truth is abyss. So is the patchy business of fallacies. Let us undone the complexities into soothe and simplistic entities.

No doubt, the post-Marx interpretations chose to focus revolution as an attempt to take hold of state, leaving aside the journey of society in cohesion and unison with the socialist republics. Yet, the historical materialism, the essence of the political dimensions of Marxism needs to be revisited from philosophical perspective, given the transformation as a step between revolutions and evolutions. This is the point, where disconnect between political left and right can be undone and a unity of opposites and diversity can be created. It will also help not only creating a patchwork between the democratic world and despotic skewed world of previously socialist states like China, Cuba, Vietnam and others in an appropriate transition into a new mode of economy that can smoothly sail amid industrialist world without invoking a conflict of interest, and thereby opening up the new ways of a polity, economy, society and international engagement for the globalized human society, with highly changed characteristics and emergence of new classes. This approach, if seen in the perspective of

Marxism, is a post Deng Xiao Pieng development in terms of polity and economy and post Lenenist development in the perspective of state and polity. This no doubt, will give a full stop to unacceptable political and economic modus oprendi of controlled and extraordinarily nationalized economies and societies. This will also help creating cushions against economic recessions around the globe by created consensual economic interdependence in the world.

Socialists of our era from Moscow in Russia to Moro town in Sindh, Pakistan have forgotten the basic principle of Hegelian logic and Marxian interpretation: unity of opposites. Soviet Union thought everything is contradiction, China did not. Pakistan was closer to China, but it also believed in the contradictions, not in their unity. Communist groups in Pakistan and rest of South Asia, greater in movements and pigmies in the basics, have been failure only because they never thought that there used to be a unity between and amongst the opposites. In Pakistan, left got defeated from right. Non-extremism and non-fundamentalism survives in Sindh and Balochistan because of Indus civilization.

Comrade M. N. Roy, a veteran Indian Marxist gave theory of peasants' revolution, which was adopted by Mao Zedong in China. Thus, revolution entered the Chinese scene.

Leninism said that after socialism, communism will take the stage of human history. Real politics juxtaposed, however. What happened? Retrogression from socialism to capitalism. The important questions here arise: Was there any true socialism in the world? Or historical materialism of Karl Marx was wrong? Because according to Karl Marx history has to progress ahead in spiral way – from slavery to feudalism, feudalism to capitalism, capitalism to socialism and socialism to communism. It cannot be retrogressive. What happened? Socialist Soviet Union turned into capitalist country. Socialism got refuge in capitalism. Is Marx's historical materialism valid? Or, was there no socialism in Soviet Union and other countries? This is a fundamental debate; let us have a new philosophical discourse. One should also go through the philosophical discourse of Leon Trotsky in this context. Trotsky can be the best refuge for socialists and Marxists of our times. In fact, a treatise is required on Hegelian and Marxian logic and materialism.

Age of a balance between materialism and idealism begins now, especially in the world politics of diversified interests, balance of power and collective good.

2

PAKISTAN: CHANGE OF FLAGS

Indus civilization ages seven thousand years. Pakistan is just seventy. Sindh and Balochistan together are the core of the Indus civilization that can be called Sindh civilization. Each brick of Maher Garh, a 5000 BC archeological site of Indus near the adorable Bolan hills of Balochistan was sold out by Sardar Yar Mohaamad Rind to international archeological mafia. The same was done by Al-Qaida and Taliban. Sardar Yar Mohammad Rid, a Baloch tribal was given protocol by the establishment of Pakistan. Why Pakistan has preferred seventy years of oblivion over seven thousand years of majesty? Silence can be the only answer from their side. Is Pakistan on the path of an unending anarchy of the State and society?

Sindhi and Baloch love their identity. We are happy that our identity is nurtured since seven thousand years. Sindh gave identity to Pakistan. Sindh Legislative Assembly passed the resolution of Pakistan. Sindh took back its favour from Pakistan in 1946 provincial elections of British India. Pakistan mongering All India Muslim League (AIML) lost the elections of 1946 in Sindh. Sindhi nationalists in alliance with Indian National Congress formed the government. After creation of Pakistan, the word and authorities of 'legislative' is omitted from Sindh Legislative Assembly in Pakistan. It is called Sindh Assembly today. Its sovereignty is intruded.

Pakistan was created on August 14, 1947 on the basis of Muslim nationhood in Indian Subcontinent, which was undone practically in 1970s by turning East Pakistan into Bangladesh on the ethnic-nationhood lines. There has been not constitution of Pakistan made by a constitutional assembly; therefore Pakistan remained under India Act of 1935 until 1950s. Pakistan adopted AIML *'Qarardad-e-Maqasid'* as preamble and essence of all would be constitution. This *'Qarardad-e-Maqasid'* led Pakistan towards Islamic state. Pakistan was not an Islamic republic on August 14, 1947. Until 1960s, judiciary and legal fraternity in Pakistan were using Indian Penal Code (IPC), Criminal Procedure Code (CrPC) and other Indian laws. Although the All India Muslim League (AIML) was rejected by the popular Will of Sindhi in 1946 and Pakistan Resolution passed by Sindh Legislative Assembly was undone.

The word 'Pakistan' was coined by Chaudhry Zafar, a London based student of Ahmadiya Muslim origin. The partition of Punjab and its becoming Pakistan could only become possible when Punjab Legislative Assembly passed resolution for the partition of Punjab and India from Punjab Legislative Assembly with one vote majority given by a Christian Punjabi.

Mohammad Ali Jinnah (M. A. Jinnah) was medically killed. He had acute asthma. His native town Jhirak was having a Tuberculosis Sanitarium and was declared a human settlement suitable most in Sindh for the rehabilitation of Tuberculosis and asthma patients. Jinnah was sent to Ziarat in Balochistan in high altitude mountains highly inappropriate for Jinnah. Jinnah in fact was born in a home on banks of river Indus in Jhirak village of district Thatta; however Pakistan history wrongly mentions that he was born in Karachi. When Jinnah had serious asthma attack, his sister Fatima Jinnah took him to Karachi for medical treatment. None received him at Karachi airport excepting the driver of a Red Cross ambulance sent by the Government. The ambulance was not even having adequate fuel. While heading for the hospital, the ambulance suddenly stopped. The driver asked Fatima Jinnah, sister of Jinnah, the founder and father of Pakistan, please take care of Qaid-e-Azam *(Great Leader--title for Jinnah)* until the fuel is arranged for ambulance. Jinnah breathed his last in the ambulance while on road. Jinnah, a Sindhi, no doubt is the first Sindhi martyr in Pakistan.

Fatima Jinnah, a Sindhi founding figure of Pakistan and sister of Mr.Jinnah, was termed a traitor and Indian agent by Pakistan Army Chief, President General Ayub Khan. Her official title in Pakistan was 'Madar-e-Milat' – mother of the nation. She was the first Sindhi and Pakistani that was dubbed an Indian agent. When mother of the nation and founding figure of Pakistan is termed traitor and Indian agent by the Chief Chowkidar (head of security), Pakistan Army Chief, labeling of Indian agents on the Sindhi, Baloch and others is meaningless.

Jinnah was married to a Zoroastrian girl, which never got converted to Islam. Jinnah was a Shi'ite Khuwaja

13

Ismaili. He in his first speech to Pakistanis termed citizens of all religions equal to the state in Pakistan. He, in his speech to the Legislators in Pakistan in 1947, said that time and history would decide whether act of creating Pakistan was right or wrong. The speech got published in Daily Republica on August 14, 2012, Opinion page.

It is important to mention here that Mahatma Gandhi was killed by Nathu Ram Godse because Gandhi was observing hunger strike against Nehru led Indian government because it was not handing over the partitioned treasury to Pakistan. Why Pakistan has not claimed Gandhi a martyr for Pakistan, if not of Pakistan. Gandhi wanted to visit Pakistan without a visa. He was never facilitated. No doubt, it was Khan of Kalat (King of Balochistan) who as the ruler of independent and sovereign Balochistan handed over money and gold to Pakistan for running its business. Balochistan was freed by Britain as sovereign country in March 1947, three months before the creation of Pakistan and partition of India.

It is a fact that Sindhi, Baloch, Pashtun, and Siraiki ethnic nations and Christians, Ahmadyas and Shia are paying worst price in Pakistan. Siraki still wait for their recognition. Pakistani manual passport is in English, Urdu and Arabic languages. English is official language of Pakistan. Urdu is lingua franca. There is no Arabian territory in Pakistan. Why, then, Arabic is published on Pakistani passports? Why not the national languages of the provinces and historical lands are recognized as national languages? Sindhi, for example, is recognized a scheduled / national language in India. USA Congress had also a decision for the development of Sindhi language. No indigenous langue is declared national language in Pakistan. In Pakistan, the website of Sindh Government is not allowed to carry Sindhi language. Balochi, Pashto, Siraiki, Punjabi and other languages are not allowed to have their official scripts. In fact Pakistani Punjabi chose the partition of pre-partition Punjab and withdrew their language as medium of education.

If Muslim is nationhood in Pakistan, whose citizens would the Christians, Zoroastrians, Ahamadiya and Jews would be? If Muslim armed forces of Islamic Republic of Pakistan, for example, fight against the Muslim armed forces of Islamic Republic of Iran and Afghanistan, whose killed soldiers would be martyrs? When the armies would chant the war-warmer slogans like 'Allah-o-Akbar' (God is great) from any of the side, whose Allah (God) would be great? Pakistan passport mentions 'Pakistani' in the column of nationality. Why, then, obsolete song of two-nation theory be sung on the both banks of Indus?

Nature of rule in colonial India; international politics in the first half of twentieth century; sudden concept of Pakistan after Second World War; and the feudalist-cum-religion orientated composition as well as politics of All India Muslim League (AIML) turned the newly created Pakistan an inappropriate statehood that has not become as yet an inclusive, people-oriented and self-relying state internally and externally.

Pakistan faced and is still facing serious constitutional crises, which is deeply rooted in the absence of the legitimate constitution until now. First two-decade long period of Pakistan was guided by Britain Indian Act of 1935, in the light of *Qaradad-e-Maqasid*, an AIML resolution adopted immediately after creation of Pakistan. After the dismemberment of Pakistan in 1971, the remaining country was limited to Indus plains. A new constitution was adopted 1973, albeit by the same Parliament that was controversial because East Pakistan's mandate was not accepted. In accordance with the political principles, practices and precedence, a non-constitutional parliament cannot undertake the constitution making process. In the perspective of federations and ethnically diverse countries, particularly if the federating states / provinces have historical status of countryhood, a constitutional elections are required which either have equal seats from the federating states / provinces or may undertake the constitutional process in association with central-provincial joint deliberations for the constitution making.

History of federating provinces in Pakistan is peculiar to federal issues. Khyber Pakhtunkhuwa (N.W.F.P previously) led by Ghaffar Khan, known as Bacha Khan, did not want to become part of Pakistan. Besides, N.W.F.P was leased out from Afghanistan for its annexation with British India through a simple Durand Agreement. Although the expiry of lease and claims of Afghanistan on Khyber Pakhtunkhuwa have been the issues that need detailed discussion, Awami National Party (ANP) is having Pashtun opinion on the historical as well as contemporary matters. Punjab chose its own split / partition into two through Punjab Legislative Assembly Resolution.

Sindh took part in the Second World War under the leadership of Pir Pagara Syed Sabghatullah Shah Rashidi known as Soorihya Badshah. The combatants were kept in prisons and also some of them were hanged after creation of Pakistan. Since Pakistan Armed Forces were created out of Punjab Regiment of British Indian Army; Air Force, Parachute Wing, Sindh-Rifle (Pakistan Rangers today), and British Navy, the armed forces of Pakistan were dominated by Punjabi Muslim soldiers, officer with a few Hindko Hazara amongst them. Even the Major General Wisal Mohammad, officer British Indian Army and Air Martial Asghar Khan, officers British Indian Air Forces, who bombed Sindh and participated offense on Sindhi by colonial Britain in the Second World war, were promoted to the posts of senior hierarchy of Pakistan Armed Forces. Since, Sindhi were not leading Sindh Intelligence during colonial Britain, which during the Second World War was led by British Army's Colonel Yung, no Sindhi and Baloch was included in the Intelligence Bureau under Prime Minister Liaqat Ali Khan. Later on they were not given spaces in the newly found Inter Services Intelligence (ISI) and Military Intelligence (MI).

Sovereignty of federating province is not recognized. Punjab protects its borders with India through Pakistan Rangers-Punjab in which Punjabi are majority. About seventeen districts of Punjab are ethnic Siraiki but they are not given adequate share in Pakistan Rangers – Punjab. Pashtuns of Khyber Pakhtunkhuwa (KP) protect their borders with Afghanistan and China through Frontier Constabulary – KP. A small number of Baloch and majority of Pashtuns protect Balochistan borders with Afghanistan and Iran through Frontier Constabulary – Balochistan. Pakistan Navy and Pakistan Coast Guards in Balochistan is Punjabi. Punjabi protect Sindh border with India through Pakistan Rangers – Sindh. Pakistan Navy and Pakistan Coast Guards in Sindh is Punjabi. Sindhi are nonexistent in Sind Regiment. Sind Regiment yet has to change its name to Sindh Regiment. 'H' in the spelling of Sind Regiment has not been added as yet even after eighteenth constitutional amendment. Baloch Regiment hardly has recruited a few Baloch very recently. Pakistan Army's other sections does not have Sindhi, Baloch, and Siraiki and to certain extent Pashtun. Similarly Inter-Service-Intelligence (ISI) and Military Intelligence (MI) do not have Sindhi and Baloch. Intelligence agencies like Intelligence Bureau (IB) although have a little recruitments of Sindhi and Baloch; however Sindhi and Baloch are not appropriately represented in this third powerful as well as civil intelligence agency of Pakistan. A true federal

Pakistan would be only when Sindhi, Baloch, Siraiki and Pashtun are appropriatly given participation in the security regime of Pakistan. It is important like Punjabis, Sindhi, Baloch and Siraiki have sovereign right to protect their international and provincial borders. A roadmap should be devised in which Sindhi, Baloch, Siraiki and Pashtun should be recruited in Pakistan Army, Pakistan Navy, Pakistan Air Force, Pakistan Coast Guard, Pakistan Rangers- Sindh, Frontier Constabulary – Balochistan and Pakistan Rangers – Punjab. Besides, their recruitment in ISI, MI, IB and FIA should also be initiated.

20

Mohammad Ali Jinnah (M. A. Jinnah), joined hands of Mohan Das Karamchand Gandhi (M.K. Gandhi) in the movement for the provincial autonomy in united India during British Raj. Pakistan was realized formally as a viable idea after 1945. The idea of Pakistan, in fact, is wrongly associated with Dr. Alama Iqbal. Dr. Iqbal basically toed the concept of amalgamation of united Punjab, Sindh, Khyber Pakhtunkhuwa (then NWFP), and Balochistan into one Muslim majority state within India. Dr. Iqbal died before the said to be Pakistan Resolution of March 23 – 24, 1940. The Resolution was not mentioning word 'Pakistan'; it was also mentioning word 'States' for the provinces. Therefore, Pakistan is post Second World War development. Besides, those legislators, led by AIML Sindh leader G. M. Syed, who presented and passed resolution from Sindh Legislative Assembly for a homeland of Muslim majority states of India quit AIML within a few years, and later on became against creation of Pakistan. They also won the provincial elections of 1946 in association with Indian National Congress and formed government in Sindh. Word 'Pakistan' was not used in the Sindh Legislative Assembly's resolution. If seen in the context of turning Sndhi people in favour of AIML; organizing it in the province; and conceiving, tabling and lobbying for the so-called Pakistan Resolution in Sindh Legislative Assembly, G. M. Syed can validly be said, if not claimed, the co-founder of Pakistan along with M. A. Jinnah. Meanwhile, according to the Pakistan Studies text books in Pakistan, when word 'Pakistan' was used for a separate country in a protest in London, it was an Idea of Ahmediya Punjabi Muslim youth. The 1946 Indian provincial elections were again a kind of referendum, in which AIML lost to those who earlier presented the Resolution from Sindh Legislative Assembly and went against it and also disassociated themselves from AIML.

21

Pakistan, created on August 14, 1947, was perceived to be a moderate secular Muslim federation by Mohammad Ali Jinnah. Jinnah was a *Kutchhi* Sindhi, born in Jhirk town of Thatta district; brought-up in Karachi, educated in London in and professionally was based in Mumbai. He was lawyer of Khan of Kalat, a King of Balochistan before creation of Pakistan.

Pakistan Resolution of 1940 was violated for the first time when Pakistan was turned from a federation of the sovereign states / provinces, against the text and spirit of 1940 Resolution, into a unitary statehood and system through 'One Unit System' by the military regime. Until 1960s, Sindh was giving financial aid to Punjab province and the central government of Pakistan, according to available documents and data. After imposing unitary system, archeological treasury of Moen Jo Daro was shifted from Sindh to Punjab, in Lahore. Replicas of the original were left in Sindh. This happened because, it was the formal colonization of other provinces in Pakistan by Punjab, which can be said internal colonization from federal perspective, because although Islamabad was the capital, Departments of Culture and Tourism as well as Water and Power (called Water and Power Development Authority – WAPDA) shifted to Lahore, the capital of Punjab. Sindhi and Bengali were the only indigenous languages that were having official scripts and were the mode of education in Sindh and East Pakistan. Writing and educating in Sindhi and Bengali was not only banned but also made a punishable offense. A punishment was also announced on writing the names of provinces anywhere including name-boards, houses, government buildings, billboards, and postal addresses. Assets of other provinces, the largest from Sindh, in terms of monetary, land, culture and reservoirs were practically handed over to Punjab province. When, Pakistan was revert back again to federal statehood, after secession of East Pakistan into Bangladesh, these assets were not given back to Sindh, Balochistan and Khyber Pakhtunkhuwa. Conspiracy was to the extent that Balochistan was asked to undo Sindhi language as mode of education in late 1960s, (until then Sindhi was mode of education of Balochistan), and was asked to adopt Urdu mode education, in lieu of which Lasbella Princely State was acceded to Balochistan, which historically was Sindh. Sindhi today have no problem with reference to Lasbella for being in Balochistan. Sindh and Baochistan are more than sister lands and have remained one country for centuries.

Sindh has deep concerns about territorial intrusions by Punjab through including Machko areas, a Sindh territory strip into Punjab province. Sindh officially have been and is demanding to stop Punjab Police and Pakistan Rangers – Punjab's violation of territorial

23

sovereignty of Sindh. No Police or military actions from the forces of Punjab should be undertaken in Sindh. Besides, all the assets, including archeological treasures, should be returned back to Sindh without any delay in accordance with the demands by Government and the people of Sindh.

The treatment of Sindh combatants of Second World War by Pakistani authorities was a violation of United Nations instruments. Pakistani Armed Forces refusal to protect borders of Sindh during 1965 War was also violation of international norms. Pakistani Armed Forces limited themselves to Punjab-India borders, particularly Lahore-Sialkot sectors, and even converted themselves into Come Cozy against the Indian tanks to protect Punjab.

Elected by the democratic system of *Hur Jammat*, Pir Pagara Syed Ali Mardan Shah became Pir Pagar, spiritual and political leader of Sindhi Hur. (*Hur* means free or liberated persons. Hur Jammat means community of free / Liberated person with hierarchy) Hur Jammat included the Second World War fighters named Hur Army / Force, was told in 1965 by Pakistan Army that military is unable to defend Sindh – India borders, therefore Pir Pagara, who was Supreme Commander Hur Army issued command for the protection and defense of Sindh. Thus, Sindh protected her borders in Pakistan with India, without participation and help by Pakistan Army. Like Suhash Chandra Bose, Pir Sabghatullah Shah Rashidi father of Pir Pagara Syed Ali Mardan Shah, is buried to unknown place. Pir Pagara Ali Mardan Shah was not allowed make thewhereabouts public. Pir Pagara probably is buried at either Astola or Churno Island near Sindh-Balochistan borders at Arabian Sea. Bose and Pir Pagara, the supreme commanders of India and Sindh during Second World War were punished because of being allies of Axis Forces. Germany, Japan, Afghanistan and Ottoman Empire supported Hur Army during Second World War; however, Hur Army was self sufficient in ammunition. Today, previous Axis Forces have allied with Allied Forces for instance US and UK alliance with Germany, Japan, and Turkey, and France. Mujtaba Rashidi, cousin of Pir Pagara Ali Mardan Shah, was central leader of Jeay Sindh Qomi Mahaz (JSQM) the largest freedom movement political party and the second largest political party in Sindh.

Sindhi and Baloch, today, like over the period of more than last one century are not part of the armed forces and services of colonial Britain and their Pakistani continuity. Even the services and forces that are created later on have been following the same footing. Sindh-Balochistan require the exclusive participation in the Sindh and Balochistan Regiments, Pakistan Rangers – Sindh, Frontier Constabulary – Balochistan, Pakistan Navy, ISI and Military Intelligence Sindh and Balochistan chapters, Pakistan Coast Guards -- Sindh and Balochistan, Intelligence Bureau Sindh and Balochistan, equal participation in remaining formations and corps of Pakistan Army and their equivalent in Pakistan Air Force, Strategic Programs like nuclear and missiles. Besides, an equal participation in Ministry of Foreign Affairs, and federal layers of Ministry of Interior, as well as other federal departments. Is it possible for Pakistan authorities that in the conflicting territories like Balochistan, the warring parties like Balochistan Liberation Army (BLA), Balochistan Republican Army (BRA) and Balochistan Liberation Front (BLF) may be engaged for negotiations and after successful negotiations can these outfits be submerged in Balochistan Regiment and other sections of Pakistan Army? A proportionate participation in the Department of Overseas Employments and other similar sections of governance are also demanded by the people of Sindh and Balochistan. At the same time, an exclusive Sindhi and

Balochistani participation in Customs, Ports, Shipping, Police, Tax collections from the Highways inclusive of Provincial taxation rights on the highways that run through Sindh and Balochistan, a non-merger of Pakistani Armed Forces in the provincial departments as well as insertion from other provinces is also required. Sindhi and Baloch have been demanding the existence of Dry Ports in Punjab should be undone, and Sindhi and Baloch should be given exclusive and priority rights in the employment of natural resources extracting companies. The private entrepreneur in the provinces should be made bound to employ locals, and permanent residents of the provinces to the greater extent. Sindhi, Baloch, Siraiki and Pashtun are under-represented in central / federal civil services. The foreign services of Pakistan hardly have a Sindhi, Baloch, Siraiki and Pashtun employees. Ninety percent overseas employment opportunities are being given to ethnic Punjabi that hail from seventeen districts of Punjab. It is essential that Sindhi, Baloch, Siraiki and Pashtun are given equal opportunities of employment in these departments.

Meanwhile, Provincial Assemblies renamed with Legislative Assemblies, with the enhanced legislative powers which must include the supervision of provincial borders, registration of internal migration from other provinces of Pakistan, and binding National Data Base Authority's (NADRA) powers with certain and concerned legislation by the provincial legislative assemblies. Sindh and Balochistan Home Departments, as well as in the others, should be entitled to issue the directions and / or unavoidable notes for the naturalization process of foreigners. This will help resisting many issues including the free movement of terrorists across the Pakistan.

Besides, Sindh and Balochistan Governments, along with others, should be given liberty to engage with the other countries even beyond the trade and business deals, particularly in terms of culture, natural disasters and similar matter if and when required accordingly.

Almost seventeen districts of Punjab in Pakistan are ethno linguistically Punjabi. The remaining seventeen are Siraiki. Southern Siraki Punjab, due to legitimate concerns of Sindh and Balochistan, should be appropriately and on the just bases be given the share within Punjab and the federation if and until Siraiki demand for a separate province is not materialized.

Chief Ministers of Sindh and Balochistan, like other Chief Ministers of Provinces, be at least virtually

28

treated like Premiers (Prime Minister of the provinces) the status that was given to them by colonial Britain, which means turning the posts of Governors into ceremonial, and Chief Ministers should be considers practically Head of the Federating Provinces / States. At the same-times, like India, if not on the patterns of UK for example the existence of Scottish Pound, the Commissionerates of Provinces should be established in Islamabad to formalized province-federation relations. Besides, a few matters / areas should be identified on which both houses of parliaments as well as provincial assemblies together may legislate.

At the same times, like India, Sindh and Balochistan, along with others, should be allowed to legislate the exclusive matters for example like in Rajasthan state of India, barrage land cannot be purchased by those who haven't got birth in Rajasthan. And, like Kashmir, no non-Kashimiri cannot purchase land in Jamu and Kashmir in India. Even a Pandit of non-Kashmiri origin cannot become the leader of religious places.

By doing this, Pakistan would be formally recognizing the sovereignty of federating provinces / states within the federation. Until and unless, provincial sovereignty is not formally and practically recognized by Pakistan (centre), Sindh and Balochistan may not consider the reviewing their will, demand and expression for freedom / secession. This means, if Self Rule inclusive of territorial as well as peoples sovereignty within the federation is not insured on above lines, Sindh and Balochistan will, according to their expressions and demands as of until 2016, will secede.

If briefed, Pakistan establishment has many layers of political and strategic decision making, governing and coordinating within and between Centre and the Provinces. For example President, Prime Minister, Chairman Joint Chiefs of Staff Committee, Chiefs of Army, Navy and Air Force, Director General of ISI, and National Security Advisor (NSA) are the core of height of establishment, constitutionally led by Prime Minister in terms of governance and by President in terms of state which also includes the decision of war making as well as use of nukes. There are two issues. One, numbers, and constitutional as well practical powers of elected civilian representation are fewer and limited respectively in the premier layer of establishment. In this layer, three are civilians, if NSA is also civilian. This also includes a Prime Minister. Remaining five are from armed forces and a services. Hence, permanent inclusion of Foreign Minister, Chief Justice of Pakistan and occasional participation of four Chief Ministers according the nature of certain decision making, including the decision for the nuclear use would give a real sense of democracy. Besides, Director General ISI as well as Head of Intelligence Bureau should be made issue based participants of this layer of the establishment. DG ISI opinion is usually shared with President of Pakistan and Chairman Joint Chiefs of Staff Committee, as well as Chief of Army Staff of Pakistan, especially the procedural and practical changes that have taken place after addition of a four-star General / Martial for the designation of Chairman Joint Chiefs of Staff Committee. Besides, the seat of Chairman Joint Chiefs of Staff Committee should also have an Air and Naval head on the seniority as well as other consideration bases.

The second tier of Pakistan Establishment, these days, is having Chief Justice of Pakistan, Chief Secretary of Pakistan, Foreign Minister, Foreign Secretary, Chairman Senate of Pakistan, Interior Minister, Director General Military Intelligence; Head of Intelligence Bureau, and occasionally is participated by the Speaker National Assembly (Lower House), Chairmen Senate Standing Committees, Heads of National Assembly Committees, Parliamentarians with special tasks, if any.

Foreign Minister should be made part of premier layer of establishment, and Foreign Secretary along with his / her team are key advisors to him; and Chief Ministers should be made Periodic part of this layer of Establishment for the efficacy and appropriate participation in terms of governance and internal security.

The third tier of the Establishment consists, federal and state Ministers, federal secretaries of various ministries / departments, and a similar participation from some other sections of the governance are party of this.

Sindh, Balochistan, and other provincial establishments are a proto-type of this; however the role of Governors and Corpse Commanders of Pakistan Army is key in the most of important matters, however Chief Ministers and Home Ministers, are part of the first layers of Provincial establishment with issue based participation of Director General Pakistan Rangers – Sindh; provincial heads of intelligence services, and Inspector General of Sindh Police. Chief Justice is not a permanent part of provincial establishment anywhere in the provinces. The second layer of provincial establishment is periodic, with participation of provincial ministers, provincial secretaries, relatively frequent participation by the heads / representation of intelligence services and similar others. Practical arrangements are different in Punjab, and to certain extent in Khyber Pakhtunkhuwa due to military operation in Federally Administered Tribal Areas (FATA) and other parts of Khyber Pakhtunkhuwa. In Punjab, practical role of Chief Minister is of Head not only of Governance but also of the province. Besides, Punjab Chief Ministers much before eighteenth constitutional amendments held agreements with the representations of other countries directly. Besides, Punjab Chief Minister has more influence in central affairs, including foreign policy and security, whilst rests have almost non-existent. This is because; ethnic establishment of Pakistan is predominantly Punjabi in almost all of its structures.

Meanwhile, Hindu, Christians, Shia and other minorities should also be given proportionate / appropriate share in the security and governance establishment, which today is almost non-existent. Besides, Sindh, Balochistan and other provinces Chief Justices should also be practically made part of provincial establishments.

Since Sindh, like Balochistan, have never been consulted on the foreign affairs and policies of Pakistan since 1947, and Sindhi and Baloch, like Siraiki and Khyber Pakhtunkhuwa people, do not have their due share in the Ministry of Foreign Affairs, therefore foreign policy of Pakistan should be considered the policy of Punjab. Therefore, all foreign policy related affairs; exclusively those to which Sindh, Balochistan and others are direct parties should be undertaken with Provincial consent. This includes, the Indus Water Treaty inclusive of Kabul River matters, Seer Creek, the regional and international climate change initiatives, borders affairs -- both provincial and international, existence of foreign forces on the land(s), water and air of Sindh and Balochistan, and others should be decided with consent by the concerned provincial governments. Sindh and Balochistan believe in the doctrine of national security and sovereignty inclusive of people along with the territory. Sindh and Balochistan promote this for the better world tomorrow.

G. M. Syed said, "Sindh is a historical country; nation; and the freedom of Sindh is possible", and can be claimed unavoidable. Sindh is also a Sovereign state. Sindh state has evolved through thousands years of

34

Kingdoms / Emirate and finally modernized under colonial Britain like united India, after having more than a dozen treaties and instruments signed between Sovereign Kingdom of Britain and Emirate of Sindh. Simultaneously, the Khanate of Balochistan had at least one Sovereign Treaty with the Kingdom of Britain. The self rule to Sindh and Balochistan, as well as others, if not liberation, will not only serve the interests of 200 million citizens across the Indus lands in Pakistan, it will also ensure the peace and security in South Asia, and will ensure global security and legitimate international stakes and interests.

3

COLONIAL SOUTH ASIA

After the dismemberment of Pakistan in 1971, and defeat in war with India, Pakistan Army launched a military operation in Balochistan. Zulfikar Ali Bhutto neither gave orders for Balochistan operation, nor did he tender suggestion for the military action in East Pakistan (now Bangaldesh). It is, thus propagated by the military and security regime of Pakistan that it was Bhutto who wanted military action in East Pakistan. The Track II and people-to-people diplomacy carried with Bangladesh during and after the period of President General Pervez Musharaf and President Asif Ali Zardari, the foreign office establishment of Pakistan, as well as their chorines vociferously mentioned Zulfikar Ali Bhutto as a sole culprit behind

1971 war on East Pakistan. This was being done in bid to attain better ties with Awami League, closer ties with Bangladesh National Party. They did not mention the role of Jamait-e-Islami Pakistan.

President Asif Ali Zardari tendered apology to Balochistan as head of the state as well as Supreme Commander of Pakistan Army. Meanwhile, President General Pervez Musharaf extended his feelings and expressions of regret to Bangladesh over 1971 war despite tendering a formal apology that was demanded by Shiekh Hasina, Bangladeshi Prime Minister.

Pakistani officials were of the opinion that by the 2016 that India is interfering in Balochistan. Previously President General Zia ul Haq regime in 1980s was saying that India is supporting Sindh. It has been a cornerstone of Pakistan's internal policy towards dissenters in Sindh and Balochistan that "external interference" be quoted as reason behind the dissent. If seen through established international practices, an interference and intervention in the affairs of a sovereign country particularly in term of civil wars and secessionism can only be validated if a) a country engages militarily in a territory, b) citizens of the country formally become part of violent conflict as soldiers, and c) weapons, specifically heavy and strategic weaponry is facilitated to the dissenters. In the context of India, neither Indian armed forces nor citizenry for war making has entered against the state of Pakistan for the freedom of Sindh and Balochistan. No weapons by India have been dispatched by India to Sindh and Balochistan.

If seen with references to international practices and precedence, European Union directly supplied heavy weaponry including strategic arsenal to Libyan rebels, almost similar happened in Syria. Even the peaceful movements like Tahreer Squire in Egypt attained equal response from across the globe, particularly by the West, which was non-violent disposition of the social action based on political will. If viewed in the perspective of the foreign policy expressions, USA and UK concerns for human rights, civil war, and Pakistan policies towards core issues concerning people of Sindh and Balochistan have been indicative of the state apparatus and constitutional crises in Pakistan. The recent statement of Indian Prime Minister Narendra Modi on Balochistan, and his December 28, 2007 statement on Sindh, one day after the murder of Benzair Bhutto, has been an expression of India on its historical legitimacy and justification. Pakistan, India and Bangladesh have remained one state although there has been no commonwealth of Indian subcontinent. During 1980s, Indra Gandhi discussed and tabled a resolution in the Lok Sabha, a lower house of Indian parliament, on Sindh against the brutalities on Sindhi. The house unanimously passed it. India, which previously refused to talk on Balochistan in a United Nations session, is now engaging with UN on Balochistan.

Sindh and Balochistan have transformed themselves into a modern nationhood, because of their historical nation and countryhood, and partly because Pakistan has failed to transform and cement into one nation. It is a fact that Britain invaded India, Sindh, Balochistan, Punjab, Sri Lanka and Myanmar as independent and sovereign countries. Khyber Pakhtunkhuwa, and some other Pashtun parts were taken from Afghanistan after failure in invasion of Afghanistan, meanwhile Bahawalpur State and Siraiki semi tribal areas adjoining to Bahawalpur State came under Britain after an agreement between Bahawalpur and Birtain. Britain military could not invade Afghanistan and Nepal. Nepal is the only South Asian country that never has been invaded in its whole history.

During earlier period of British invasion Tamil that were indigenous to India bordering Sri Lanka received further migration of Tamil from India for labouring in tea farms. Colonial Britain freed India, Myanmar and Sri Lanka with the sovereignty of independent country in which these were invaded. Balochistan was also freed by annexing Pashtun area of Afghanistan five months before the partition of British India. Punjab chose its division / partition through legislature. Khyber Pakhtunkhuwa was annexed with Pakistan against the will of its elected government. Afghanistan was not taken into discussion regarding this. Bahwalpur State, against the agreement between King of Bahawalpur and the Britain, in which Bahawalpur was guaranteed security from invasion by Punjab, was annexed with Punjab along with other Siraiki areas.

Sindh was invaded by Britain through violation of various Treaties, which were reached upon after negotiations, and were accorded by emissaries of Her Excellency Queen of Britain that ensured British security to Sindh from invasion of Punjab. Against the sprit of these treaties, Sindh on August 14, 1947 was annexed with newly created Pakistan. Besides, the Will of Sindhi who voted against AIML in 1946 was also violated. Punjab, no doubt, in 1930s sent a proposal to

40

the Governor General of India that Sindh should be annexed with Punjab because it is Muslim majority adjoining territory, which was opposed by G. M. Syed, Mohammad Ali Jinnah, Sir Shah Nawaz Bhutto, Jamshed Nasarwanji Mehta, Haji Abdullah Haroon, and by other Sindhi politicians. Britain refused Punjab its request for annexing Sindh with Punjab.

Sindh was invaded by Britain during 1843-1857. Not only the agreements that were made by Britain before 1843 with Sindh were violated, also Government of Sindh, Primer of Sindh, and the Cabinet of Sindh were not taken into consultation for its annexation into a newly proposed country – Pakistan. Balochistan, however, was formally taken into control by Pakistan in 1948. Mir Ghouse Bux Bijanzo was the Parliamentarian in the bicameral parliament of Balochistan, who led the majority opposition against Mohammad Ali Jinnah's proposal for annexation of Balochistan with Pakistan. Government of Pakistan sought vote from Quetta Municipality, a local government body of Quetta city, in fvaour of Pakistan.

The historical affinity between Baloch and Pashtun of Balochistan has many examples. Marriage of a Khan (King) of Kalat was from the family of a Prince in

Kandahar, Afghanistan, who gifted Quetta to her daughter as *Shaal (a cultural gift)*. Government of Pakistan said that borders security, international affairs, and currency would be Pakistan Governments responsibility, rest the Governance of Balochistan would be of locals. Judiciary in Balochistan later on was submerged with traditional tribal judicial mechanism; Nawabs (Princes) and Sardars (Dukes) were recognized right of policing and levying tax through Levies; and Baloch were allowed to hold weaponry without licenses. Baloch fought many wars began around in decade of its annexation with Pakistan. A truce was reached through traditional use of Holy Koran with Shaheed Nawab Nauroz Khan, and later on the truce was violated.   The ongoing war in Balochistan is underway since last seventeen years.

Government of Sindh and Government of Khyber Pakhtunkhuwa were dismissed in 1948 and 1947 respectively because both of the governments, primarily opposed the annexation with Pakistan, and after creation of Pakistan, wanted an entirely different kind of federalism. Leadership of Sindh and Balochistan during last seven decades was killed, mostly by the Pakistan armed forces. Sindh, through Sindh Assembly and representation in federal parliament as well as through popular protest of public; and Balochistan through massive protests and warfare have been protesting regarding people's security, sovereignty, self rule and autonomy, besides demanding for secession.

Balochistan during the military rule of President Genral Pervez Musharf was demanding sovereign autonomy of Balochistan, and the same momentum, however peaceful, has been there in Sindh and Khyber Pakhtunkhuwa which also include the demand for the freedom of Sindh. Siraiki have been demanding a separate Siraiki province through Parliament and streets. Balochistan and Sindh freedom movements, in association with war in Balochistan, have been oldest in the history of Pakistan if compared with liberation movement of Bangladesh.

There has been freedom movement in Gilgit and Baltistan areas in Pakistan for the creation of Blaveristan. Gilgit and Baltistan historically are parts of Kashmir and were invaded by in 1947-48 war on Kashmir. Meanwhile, terrorists belonging to Salafi sects went inroads in the area to resist Khuwaja Shi'a Ismaili majority of Gilgit-Baltistan. The spiritual leader of Khuaja Shia Ismaili, His Highness Prince Agha Khan, is also a leader of Gilgit-Baltistan. He is a Sindhi, born on the banks of River Indus in Jhirik town of district Thatta. Once, during His Highness visit of Karachi he said, , "I am soul of Sindh." This very same statement was given by veteran Sindhi Leader Rasool Bux Palijo and Pir Pagaro Syed Ali Mardan Shah. Sindh Government felt honored by His Highness Prince Agha Karim Khan's visit of Chief Minister House Sindh during which Sindh Government requested Abida Parveed to perform Ganaya in the honour of His Highness.

44

4

SOCIOLOGICAL POLITY

Sindhi and Baloch today have transformed into **45** modern social and cohesive entities, as they were historically however the linguistic, ethnic and sub-cultural additions that were resulted by the Partition of British India, (after the creation of Pakistan) initiated the process of integration in the societies. Politics is patchy social process, imbibed with the power; therefore state apparatus of Pakistan, like elsewhere in the world today, has particularly determined the social interdependence among and between the indigenous-aboriginal Sindhi and Baloch as well as the migrants, refugees, and immigrants between 1947 and 2016.

Nationhood, nationality, and identity today are diversified, as well as simple matters. This can only be described, determined, categorized and awarded on the grounds of aboriginality, indegenioushood, ethnicity, linguistics, ethnology particularly in contemporary world of post-immigration and migration issues, United Nations instruments, comprehensive laws and procedures practiced in the nation-states and federations across the globe.

In Sindh, Kolhi, Bhil, Meghwar, Rebari, Gurgla and Brahvi, the aboriginal Dravidians and Proto-Dravidians; and *Sammat* specifically and rest of original Sindhi are indigenous. *Samaat* mainly includes Arians, Brahman Hindus, various lineages of Rajputs, the communities associated with Indus and died River Sarswati, lakes and waters bodies, cost and islands. *Non-samaat* indigenous Sindhi include ethnic and / or linguistic Balochi who claims Sindhi identity are indigenous Sindhi that includes indigenous Siraki subculture of Sindhi as well. This also includes those who settled in Sindh over one century. Indigenous Sindh is majority in Sindh.

Indigenous Sindhi, who earlier were living in the 1700s borders of Sindh, and later on moved in the contemporary and Britain borders of Sindh, for examples Kutchi, and some other *Zaats*[1] are aboriginal or indigenous Sindhi. Indigenous Baloch of Karachi who claim Baloch identity are also indigenous Sindhi with their Baloch identity. Baloch that have migrated to Sindh from 1890 to 1945 are submerged in Sindhi society, and cannot be thought of being non-indigenous. Thus, by every mean they are considered indigenous and original Sindhi with their elders Baloch identity. Punjabi who migrated to Sindh after the commissioning of Sukkur, Guddu and Kotri Barrages (Ghulam Mohammad Barrage) have assimilated in Sindh, therefore they are Sindhi and can be said Sindhi of Punjabi origin. Some amongst them are still holding Punjabi sub-culture, especially those who migrated after commissioning of Kotri Barrage and Guddu Barrage; however their large majority has submerged linguistically with Sindhi. A smaller numbers of Rajasthani and Gujarati in various districts on the western bank of Indus as well as in the cities of Karachi, Hyderabad, Thatta, and southern parts of district Jamshoro that includes Memon of Okhai and Kutyana background, Silawat, and other *Zaats* are also

47

---

[1] The family lineage on the pattern of profession, topography, and iconic family backgrounds.

Sindhi, and using either various dialects of Sindhi or a blend of Sindhi-Rajasthani or Sindhi-Gujarati. Most of them, like Memon, are from within the historical borders of Sindh. Smaller groups like Silawat who settled in Sindh on the invitation of Pir Pagar Surihya Badshah in 1900s, and others who either have migrated before partition of India from various cultures and lands of Southasia, or during the Britain India, have not only assimilated in Sindh and with Sindhihood, but also have been protecting and defending Sindh. It is general unwritten rule of Sindhi that indigenous and migrant Baloch are Sindhi in Sindh.

Sindhi at the border with Rajasthan and Gujarat state of India speak Sindhi, Dhatiki, Marwari, and Parkari. Sindhi in Rajasthan, India particularly Barmer and Jaisalmir districts, speak Sindhi, Dhatki and Marwari. On the both side of the borders, people are indigenous in overwhelming majority. Meanwhile, districts of Kutch and Bhuj in Gujarat, India are ethno-linguistically Kutchhi Sindhi Muslims and are indigenous majority in the districts. Rest of Sindhi dictions and their spoken centers are *Laari Lasi*[2] in

---

[2] **Sindhi diction**

Karachi; *Laari*[3] and *Laari* Lasi Thatta; *Laari* in Badin; Mirpurkhas; Tando Allahyar, and Tando Mohammand Khan. Although *Laari*, but called literary Sindhi, is spoken in Hyderabad, and adjoining Jamshoror and Kori towns and villages, as well as in Matyari districts. *Lari Lasi* is also spoken between river Indus to the borders with Balochistan downward Jamshoro and Kotri towns of district Jamshoro, and Jhirik of district Thatta. *Wicholi*[4], which has no popular name, is spoken in Nawabshah, Dadu, northen Jamshoro and Naushehro Feroz. *Utaradi*[5], is spoken in Khairpur, Larkana, Sukkur, Ghotki, Kashmore, Jaccobabad and Qambar-Shahdadkot districts of Sindh. Siraiki, is not an alien language of Sindh. Sindhi rulers during first half of 1800s were Sindhi of Siraiki dialect. They ruled Sindhi until invasion of Sindh in 1843.

Linguistically Siraiki is diction of Sindhi, its name is acquired from Sindhi word *Siro*, which means 'the fringe' in Sindhi. Siraiki means language that is spoken at the fringes of Sindh in north. Multan has once remained capital of the Kingdom of Sindh. The ethnic composition of Siraki people is like Sindhi and Baloch,

49

---

[3] Sindhi diction
[4] Sindhi diction
[5] Sindhi diction

a blend of ethnic Baloch, Sindhi of *Samat* (indigenous) and Dravidian (aboriginal) origin. They form ethno-linguistically half of population in Punjab

Indian Partition refugees, however their offspring are sons and daughters of the soil and are Urdu speaking, Bihari (Bhaujpuri mostly), and Qaimkhani (Rajasthani) Sindhi. The process of their integration with indigenous Sindhi majority is underway in Sindh, albeit very slow paced in terms of sociological inter-weaving.

In some cases, those ethnically or linguistically non-Sindhi, have migrated towards Sindh since 1990, and have become permanent residents of Sindh, have no intention to return to their lands, and have associated their interests and commitments with Sindh in terms of its sovereignty and security in all of its manifestations, can be said and claimed as Sindhi. However, as rule of thumb, and in the light of United Nations instruments, the offspring of migrants are also Sindhi. It is an unwritten and consensual sentiment and expression of Sindhi that those who does not pour their commitment with the sovereignty, security and interest of Sindh, can never be accepted as Sindhi.

In Balochistan, Baloch of Balochi group of languages that include Proto-Dravidian Brahvi; various versions, dialects and expressions of Balochi spoken in the cultural-topographical areas of Sarawan, Jhalwan, Makaran, and Sindhi (Lasi and Utradi) are the indigenous and aboriginal Baloch.

Aboriginal as well as indigenous Sindhi including Lasi Lari Sindhi, Utradi and other smaller variant linguistic groups of Balochi including Brahvi are mostly dwelling at the borders with Sindh, Iran and Afghanistan, and Siraki areas of Punjab. This also includes those who are living in Afghanistan (Helmand province) and Iran (Sistan-Balochistan province) and speak Balochi and Sindhi.

Pashtun are aboriginal and indigenous in Balochistan. There are refugees and migrant (from Afghanistan) Pashto speaking Balochistani. Previously known as British Balochistan, the Pashtun area of Balochistan is similar to Balochi. Almost similar in patterns, tribal construct and principles. The historical affinity between Baloch and Pashtun has many examples like the one, marriage of a Khan of Kalat from the family of Prince in Kandahar, who gifted Quetta to her daughter as *Shaal* (a cultural gift). Pashto speaking areas of Balochistan include the Afghanistan-Pakhtukhuwa-FATA bordering tribal, the high rise mountainous, and

51

valley areas. Pashto in Balochistan is linguistically associated with southern Afghanistan Pashto with its own peculiarities, and dialectical waves amongst bordering tribal and valley Pashtun. Pashtun refugee influx from southeastern Afghanistan particularly from the area that falls between Qandahar to Zabul during the Cold War has been witnessed in the districts adjoining to Quetta.

Baloch and Pashtun share historically, culturally and linguistically one common city, Quetta, where Pashtun are aboriginal, and linguistic Brahvi and Balochi Baloch are indigenous. Khuzdar, the second largest city of Balochistan, is Baloch of linguistic Brahvi and Balochi residents.

During 1970s and later on, the anarchy in Afghanistan mainly became reason to larger migration of Persian speaking Hazara from central Afghanistan. Hazara, historically, are ethnic Mongolian. They almost are limited to Quetta city with a smaller number of populations in comparison with Pashtun and Baloch in Quetta. The settlement patterns of Pashtun, Baloch and Hazara are similar to certain extent; however the development and urbanization in Quetta, although slow paced, has changed the ethnic patterns of settlements. Unlike the Pashtun residents of city, the oldest one, and the Pashtun and Brahvi settlers in the rural orchards of the urban Quetta are now urbanized Baloch parts of the city. The returnee of Balochistan Liberation War mostly from Helmand, who returned with the comeback of Nawab Khair Bux Murri, their tribal and political leader, are settled in the worst living condition outside Quetta on the sides of Ring Road. No displacement support has been tendered to them, over one decade, either from Government of Balochistan, Quetta Municipality, and the UNHCR. They live in the temporary hamlets.

53

The understanding, historically between the people from Sindh and Balochistan, and officially between Governments of Sindh and Balochistan is that the rainfall on the bordering mountains, if and where it drains towards Balochistan is the area of Balochistan, and if and where it drains to Sindh is the area of Sindh.

Sindhi speaking Baloch resides in Lasbella where they are known as *Lasi,* and the language is called Lasi or Lasi Lari. Baloch of historical *Magus* Area, called Jhil Magsi, mostly speak a Sindhi blended with Balochi or Balochi blended with Sindhi. Baloch of Dera Allahyar, Dera Murad Jamali, Sibi and Bolan speak Balochi as well as Sindhi. Similar patterns are also found to certain extent in the various pockets of Khuzdar and Kalat. Brahvi are Balochi Dravidians, who live in Balochistan and Sindh indigenously. Linguistically Brahvi and Sindhi until mid 1980s shared around 30 percent vocabulary at least. Brahvi and Tamil language also share phonetics and considerable vocabulary. Various dialects of Balochi are spoken in the cultural-topographical areas of Balochistan, and have a better linguistic connectivity with Persian at the Iran borders particularly in southeastern Balochistan. Baloch of Helmand, Afghanistan are Balochi speaking, while Baloch of Sistan-Balochistan, Iran and adjoining areas speak Sindhi blended with Persian influenced Balochi, and Iranian Balochi. *Jadgal* [6] form majority in Sistan-Balochistan in Iran. They are recognized Baloch in Iran and in Balochistan.

Sindhi of all faiths and paths, reside in all continents. There are Sindhi that are historically submerged in some nations, like in Kingdom of Saudi Arabia, Sindhi who are now indigenized there with the tribe or clan name Al-Sindi. Some Sindhi families are submerged in Java and Sumatra islands; and some are submerged in

54

---

[6] **Linguistically non-Balochi, but ethnically Baloch**

Russia, living in Moscow having combination of names and family names of Sindhi and Russian. They migrated from Sindh in 1800s. There are indigenized Sindhis in various African countries. A large number of Sindhi live in Diaspora after partition of united India, and thereafter during last seven decades are in Europe, Asia Pacific, Middle East, Africa, and North America. Sindhi are indigenized in Afghanistan with 15000 population, some villages of Sindhi are there in Chittagong and Khulna Divisions of Bangladesh where they are indigenized. Sindhi are second largest business community after Jews in the world, which includes those who directly migrated from Sindh to various countries, and those who routed the travel from India. This still is happening. Besides, an exodus of Sindhi Hindu due to the harassment caused in 1948 by non-Sindhi and thereafter is taking place towards India and some other countries.

Dutch were the first among the European nations that colonized South Asia. Goa in India and Gundz between Gawadar and Pasni on the Balochistan coast were the areas of this region that were inhabited by Dutch. Britain came later. Dutch colonizers settled in Gundz and submerged in Baloch nation, and are called Dutch Baloch.

55

Sindh and Balochistan, for centuries, have remained one country, with combined capitals and headquarters in Kalat, Hyderabad, Sukkur, Brihamanabad and Multan during various periods of the history. Southern Punjab, the Siraiki land, has also remained part of that Kingdom for centuries, and shared common centre of Indus civilization, which earliest was centered in Meher Garh (5000 BC). The adjoining districts to Meher Garh in Balochistan, are Balochi, and link Sindhi speaking Baloch plains of Balochistan. First excellence in Urbanization of human history, Moen Jo Daro (3000 BC) is located in the centre of Sindh on the right bank of river Indus. Indus Civilization or Sindh Civilization has its spread up to Tibet in China in the north; eastern Afghanistan and Kandahar; Gujarat and Rajasthan states of India and in Haryana state, and has its borders in the east up to Cambodia. Between Myanmar to Cambodia, it infuses with Yellow river civilization of China, therefore, historically and academically this area is called Indo-China.

The Indus civilization has another city Harapa, in Punjab of Pakistan; however the capital of the civilization, Moen Jo Daro (Sindh), because of being on the Banks of river Indus and near the Sea, is exceptionally urbanized due to being trade centre of the civilization.

Indus civilization has hundreds of Indus sites in Kutch, Bhuj, more than that of in Sindh. In that context, the hitherto held researches proves that Kutch, Bhuj, and some other areas of Gujarat in India have more Indus sites if compared with Sindh, Balochistan, Punjab, and elsewhere. In Gujarat new excavations of the sites were successfully undertaken by 2013; however the excavations in Gujarat are also under process. Besides, one Indus site was discovered by 2012-2013 in Haryana state of India.

Indus, that begins in Tibet (in China), shares its name Sindhu with the land Sindh, which today is a federating state in Pakistan; albeit historically have remained a country for centuries. It is academically established that Moen Jo Daro was capital of Indus civilization, led by the King Priest. Apart from so many heights of urbanization, the city was having covered drainage and sanitation, and also was having a swimming pool, called Great Bath. The structure there has also arrangements of bathing norms including dressing and other necessities. It is shocking to see the civilization disconnect between Indus Civilization (Asia) and the West. Europe and North America, excluding the snowy regions, have a history of weekly bathing that was practiced until 1960s. Americans were first among the Westerns who started daily bathing in 1970s, and thereby rest of western societies followed American bathing routine. Perfumes in Europe were necessity due to this delayed bathing; hence France did mastery in putting foundations of perfume. Perfumes for decades have remained an important source of exports for France.

Sindh and Balochistan are thankful to the United States of America for its support to the Government of Sindh for being concerned and rendering support for the protection, renovation and preservation of archeological sites in Sindh through its Islamabad Embassy and Karachi Consulate. Sindh and Balochistan, once Buddhist, are also grateful to Japan for its support to Sindh to protect Indus civilization through protecting its capital, Moen Jo Daro by the means of coating it. Unfortunately, the funds released to the Government of Pakistan were not used for five years. Moen Jo Daro still requires appropriate initiatives for its protection. Sindh and Balochistan are also thankful to Russian Federation, which through Islamabad Embassy participated Moen Jo Daro initiatives by Pakistan People's Party (PPP) Chairman Bilawal Bhutto Zardari, son of great Sindhi leader martyred Benazir Bhutto. Balochistan and Sindh are also thankful to the Italy for returning back the archeological assets of Balochistan, which Italian authorities collected while acting against international mafia of archeological smugglers. Sindh and Balochistan welcome previous US President Bill Clinton's remarks on Moen Jo Daro and the people of Indus civilization during his presidential address; and also for being concerned for civilization, culture and Sufism in Sindh and Balochistan, the mainland Indus civilization.

In Sindh, Urdu speaking Sindhi and Sindhi speaking Sindhi shared differences over development, which turned into lesser than five years in low-scale violence. Gradually, it started turning into tolerance, and between 2000 and 20012 it transformed into accommodation of both.

Sindh and Balochistan together like Khyber Pakhtunkhuwa have received Afghan refugee of cold war, who lived for over a couple of decades on the lands, and a large number of them is still staying in Sindh and Balochistan. Balochistan, recently through

Sardar Mehmood Khan Achakzai said that Khyber Pakhtunkhuwa belongs to Afghan, and the Afghan refugees are rightful to live over there. The reconstruction of Afghanistan carried out by international community led and participated by USA, and other UN Security Council members, although has created conducive environment that a considerable number of Afghan refugees have returned Afghanistan until 2012.

Sindh is facing serious crises of demographic pressure in the form of refugees and illegal immigrants from across the world because Government of Sindh is not entitled to legislate, play determining role and decide the refugee status, settlement as well as naturalization of the foreigners. Balochistan and Khyber Pukhtunkhuwa are also undergoing the same situation. Punjab is the only province in Pakistan, which almost does not receive refugees. Even due to the Operation Zarb ul Azab by Pakistan Army on the insistence of USA has caused displacements, which were directed towards Sindh. Punjab refused receiving the internally displaced persons of flood in Khyber Pakhtunkhuwa, like it did during the settlement of Afghan refugees of cold war.

Sindh has cordially received Baloch displaced persons due to civil war in Balochistan. Sindh, like Balochistan, previously received Iranian refugees due to Islamist revolution in Iran. Africans including Sudanese, Nigerians, as well as Palestinians are living in Sindh including a limited number of far-eastern refugees.

Hundreds of Tibetan and a few thousand Poland (Polish) refugees got settled in Sindh between 1920 and 1940s. Some Tibetan live in Karachi. Polish have naturalized in Sindh. Besides, due to security reasons, some of Jews of Karachi have preferred to claim Zoroastrian *(Parsi)* identity. They are not counted in census. Gorkhas from Nepal are also localized in Karachi.

Hundreds of thousands Bangladeshi illegal immigrants are living in Karachi. Until 2012, 200,000 ethnic Rohengyan Muslims have illegally entered Sindh and sought refuge. The worst aspect of this is despite documenting these illegal entrants; the National Data Base Authority (NADRA), a central government agency, issues them citizenship documents within shorter span of time. Government of Sindh is not consulted for that matter. Even some illegal Afghans including the very recent ones have sought Pakistani citizenship along with the travel documents.

Sindh is already undergoing demographic issues, and peopling of Sindh has become a real challenge with reference to the people's sovereignty. Taking care of hundreds of thousands refugees since three decades and receiving the new ones, with swift citizenship facilitation, is an act of ethnic cleansing by tactically converting aboriginal, indigenous and indigenized majority into minority besides causing gradual exodus of Hindus from Sindh. Moreover, cities of Sindh cannot afford further massive influx of refugees and illegal entrants because number of immigrants and settlers from within Pakistan come in hundreds of thousands every decade. This further is intensified when Pakistani armed forces entrepreneur sector has acquired hundreds of thousand acre lands in Karachi, Hyderabad, Sukkur, and other places to develop mostly high-rise buildings for accommodating hundreds of thousands more from outside Sindh. This no doubt includes various schemes like Bahriya Town, the largest one in Karachi.

Entry of terrorists associated with Al-Qaida, ISIS and other groups has remained frequent, identified in some cases and have always been posing security risk, and threat to considerable extent. Therefore exclusive authority for settlements from within Pakistan particularly in Sindh needs the decentralization of the process of immigration, naturalization and refugee resettlement. It is needed to mention that Punjab alone in Pakistan does not have considerable number of foreigners as well as internal migrants from Sindh, Balochistan and Khyber Pakhtunkhuwa. And, Sindh alone, apart from world outside, receive hundreds of thousands from northern Pakistan, particularly from Punjab. Sindh and Balochistan have been demanding the protection of their demographic sovereignties through legislation, and procedural empowerment.

Sindh is the only federating province in Pakistan, in whose legislature recent settlers are allowed to run elections, become members of Sindh legislature and also become cabinet ministers. Sindh and Balochistan have been demanding new legislation for the vote rights in the historical lands to those who have not got birth there. The settlers' participation for the provincial and federal legislatures should be barred. After ten years of their settlement, they should be given right to run elections for the local government, and those who get birth in Sindh may be legitimize to become members of legislatures after process of elections.

During 2014 – 2016 Punjab Police, Pakistan Rangers – Punjab and Pakistan Army based in Punjab have violated sovereignty of Sindh by undertaking military actions in Sindh on the orders of Punjab government. In federations across the world, federating states or province do contribute their Sovereignty to create a Federation in the Sovereignty of Republics. There is no land or territory within Pakistan which is called Pakistan. Sindh, Balochistan, Punjab and Khyber Pakhutkhuwa together, willingly or unwillingly, form the entity named Islamic Republic of Pakistan.

In 2013, Jammat-e-Islami Pakistan declared Mohammad Bin Qasim 'First Pakistani'. Later on in 2013, Pakistan Army Chief General Pervez Kiyani while addressing the army men said that Mohammad Bin Qasim is the 'First Pakistani'. Apart from the dissents concerning historical and contemporary narratives about Pakistan, it is established fact according to the official record; the name of newly found country was 'Pakistan' in 1947. Pakistan was officially named Islamic Republic of Pakistan in 1973. It means Pakistan was not Islamic country or republic on August 14, 1947.

64

This is also validated by the speeches by M. A. Jinnah after creation of Pakistan. If this is very same Pakistan of M. A. Jinnah, then why one needs to choose First Pakistani from among the Arab invaders? Was Jinnah not the First Pakistani? Besides, how a General who leads an Army of existing country can term an invader a hero? Can a general be allowed to claim Alexander 'First Pakistani'? Sindh Balochistan, together one country Sindh at that time under Raja Dasrath, gave Alexander a tough fight; and ironically Punjab, having capital at that time between Taxila and Islamabad welcomed Alexander without any fight. If Pakistani armed forces are federal, can they claim invaders of any part in the federation of Pakistan as their hero? Holy Koran says that faith / religion is ones' personal matter. Why then, a Republic can and should be Islamic? Wasn't it the reason that Holy Prophet chose word *Khalafat* (Caliphate) despite Islamic Republic? God himself says in Holy Koran by mentioning word "nation" that waging war to defend the nation is appreciated. However, Holy Koran never suggests military offense; and the wars waged during the period of Holy Prophet were not offensive. They were either defense or defensive offense. Why not, if unavoidable and enviable, with the consent of Sindh and

65

Balochistan, and rest of the provinces and federating nations of Indus lands, Khudaijatul Kubra Allaih Sallam (A. S.), and *Hazarat* Ali A.S. chronologically first Muslims, be declared First Pakistani? One of Pashtun Saduzai, Sindhi and Baloch Asehaba Akraam should not be declared First Pakistani? A Sindhi woman was Harem in the family of Holy Prophet, why then she should not be declared first Pakistani? Imam Hussain wanted to settle in Sindh of Hindu King. Why Imam Hussain should not be declared first Pakistan? Would it not be ideological security of 'Islamic Republic'? Pakistani Passport carries word 'Pakistani' for the Nationality of the passport holders. If nationality of the people in Pakistan is Pakistani, why to claim Muslim nationhood? What about two-nation theory? Is there any formal treatise of Two Nation theory because theories are always expressed in philosophy? Besides, If Islamic Republic of Pakistan's military wages war against another Islamic Republic's army, for example Afghanistan or Iran? Both would be raising the slogan 'Allah-o-Akbar' (God is great). Whose God would be great? And, if soldiers killed, whose soldiers would be martyr?

If Mohammad Bin Qasim is the first Pakistani, Jinaah is the last.

Sindh and Balochistan do not believe in Two-Nation theory. Besides, in 1971 East Pakistan became Bangladesh on ethnic-national bases. Wasn't it the great truth of our times? Sindh and Balochistan have expressed themselves by participating Second World War for the freedom of Sindh; in 1946 British Indian provincial elections; in 1948 through Balochistan parliament, and later on until now. After dismemberment of Pakistan in 1971, Sindh and Balochistan, and Khyber Pakhtunkhuwa also were not sought their Will through election for the constitutional assembly? Thus, Sindh and Balochistan ascertain that their being part of State of Pakistan is violation of their will. Sindh and Balochistan, Khyber Pakhtunkhuwa, and Siraiki southern Punjab through their elected political representations, although their participation in Pakistan Armed Forces was negligible, never gave consent, opinion or suggestion for waging war on East Pakistan. Thus, around seventeen Punjabi speaking districts declared 1971 war on East Pakistan and on its people -- men, women, and children. Hence, Sindh and Balochistan in terms of any action by the forces of the State on the political dissent and difference on federalism is considered war against historical

67

homelands and their people in Sindh, Balochistan or elsewhere.

Sindh and Balochistan re-ascertain their sovereignty in terms of territory, people, political will, and governance including economy. Government of Sindh and Balochistan, through their Assemblies, Chief Ministers, Cabinet Ministers, political leaders, religious scholars and persons of opinion have time and against protesting and expressing their will against armed forces and services actions against people and the lands. The collective will has been expressed by the legislatures, governments, political and social leadership, and millions of people's action for taking to the streets concerning broader sovereignty and security of Sindh and Balochistan, regarding issues ranging all fields of statehood of the federating provinces. When armed forces and services actions referred to the Sindh High Court and Balochistan High Court, an attempt of justice was made. Sindh and Balochistan officially, publicly and popularly, politically and socially have been mentioning the discrimination, humiliation, intrusion and non-cooperation by Punjab in terms of economic, social and political acts and actions. Chief Minister and representation of Sindh Government also have formally mentioned the colonization of Sindh by Punjab. Government of Balochistan has time and again been expressing its opinion on Guwader and other matters and issues. This is nothing but seventy years long federal failure, to which seventy years long popular will has been expressed through all legitimate and recognized means, institutions and forums, and in last one decade reiterated in all forms as mentioned above. Sindh and Balochistan, therefore, gave option to the Islamic Republic of Pakistan to transform into a new statehood, a Union of Sates that falls around the Indus with the popular and constitutionally elected will of the historical lands, for ensuring sovereign autonomy and self rule for the historical nations and lands around the Indus. Let the foundation civilization and urbanization of humankind rooted in Sindh and Balochistan, spread across the Indus, and beyond, contribute into polity and culture of human interaction in Pakistan, South Asia and across the world.

69

5

CONTEMPORARY CIVILIZATION

Just think that God himself, the prophets and religious masters are addressing the communication and urban revolutionized world with Metropolitans, primary, secondary and tertiary cities, towns, and the globally connected countryside. How exactly would they be finding in a Metropolitan devilling boy and country side girl using communication revolution and enjoying the connectivity with the *worldmates* and *globemates*.

Contemporary civilization of us is destined end with the unity amongst us all with no doubt some differences that include development, polity, statehood, economy and culture. The connectivity of spiritual manifestations with the physical, material and humanly one, express itself into all forms of a social world outwardly and a inter being inwardly. This is called *Zuhud* (religious practices for spiritual elevations) in theology, *Juhud* (social or individual struggle with reference to religions or ideology) and social actions. In theosophy, this is a simplistic action and approach which create a wave of integration between one's social and spiritual expression as well act; however a Sufi adds a musical rhythm between inner with the outer that gives him an attached-detachment with society. No doubt, a point comes where a Sufi jumps towards climax of spirituality where *Juhud* and *Zuhud* transforms *Wujid* (climax for spiritual influence by the existence) through the oneness with God, the Absolute Being; this comes however in a trans based on a process with the Sufi practices in almost all kinds across the continents especially in Sindh, and South Asia, Middle East, Western and the rest in Africa and Asia.

Zuhud, Juhud and *Wujud* are Middle Easters terms, which have their accurate terminologies in Sindh and Balochistan, South Asia, West, China-Korea, Africa, South America and Eurasia, have new transformations in the contemporary world that include the religious influences in the post-structural as well as reformist;

71

and the influences by our contemporary civilization which primarily is based, led and rewritten by the urbanization. Urbanization today is not limited to the large and largest cities; the barriers of population, metropolitenhood, and multi-culturalism are crossing the limits of structural urbanization, and have entered into rural society through the communication revolution. This revolution is called contemporary civilization, and has transformed our world like a classical Raga is infusion and can easily be called rock-fusion of human development.

Liberation of mind, for example, has always remained the fundamental of every religion, theosophical movement and Sufi paths. It has expressions according to the space, since liberation of mind is usually an act to transcend beyond the Time. Therefore, faithful, theosophists, and Sufis artificially detach from the immediate space which is called *Tiag* in Sindhi. This is an attempt of meditative saturation, which basically equates the Time in the space, and the time inside. Which, in philosophical term, is a state of being where subjectivity attaches and equates with objectivity -- thus it's becomes a phenomenon beyond the old discussions between subjective idealism and objective subjectivism. It is state of existence, where subjectivity and objectivity detaches from the consciousness of space and creates harmony between Time within oneself and beyond. At very this juncture, theoretical philosophies becomes manifested into the practical outlook in a single entity, when a human becomes in control of the relations between Time Beyond and Time Inside -- in Time as such which can be called one's natural-self. And, space becomes relative, a detached-attachment or an existing reality that is detached in one's own perceptions and thoughts. In social terms, a person is not a liberated mind if someone in his thought at least, if not in actions in totality, transforms beyond exaggerated self, unnecessary bondages of family, clan, cast, ethnicity, nation, conservatives in ideologies and religions, irrelevant spiritual norms, certain social norms, and the *cronyism* in economy, and traditional in development as well as stagnant in polity. Liberation in its all manifestations, is only possible when a human, an existence, transients beyond these. Process for the liberation of mind is the path in itself. The liberation in Islam from the conservatively limiting everything to Islam, is "Lakum Deenakum, Wali-e Deen" which essentially means faith is one's liberty to be associated

73

with. It says, in socio-politically terms, according to Islam, religion is personal matter.

Liberation of existence from the world, according to religions beginning their journey with Vedism (Sindh) to Sanathanism (Hinduism), Buddhism, Jainism, Tao and Confucianism, Judaism, Christianity, Islam and path of Sikhism is cosmology which is not limited to the theology, it also has Sufism and philosophical expression. Contemporarily, life, its liberation and rebirth, has been challenged as well as proved through the experience of cloning.

According to Indian philosophy when a soul departs from bodily existence, and another bodily organism is ready to enter in the formal existence in the any part of universe, the departing soul, in the matrix of time and space, transforms into the upcoming being with certain more characteristics, is called the rebirth.

Therefore question of liberation is associated with the issue of rebirth in theology, which in theosophy, philosophy and Sufism has an entirely cosmological view. In the words of Hassan Dars, an icon of contemporary Sindhi poetry "He jisim hik wago aa, Panhinjo assan khe patal" (physical being is a worldly attire). Sindhi expression, even today, connects with

Vedic (Sindh), Hinduism; Confucianism; Tao, Buddhism; Jainism; Judaism; Christianity; Islam; Sikhism; philosophy of at least liberation of being of Marxism and Jean Paul Sartre; and in Southern Pakistan (Sindh, Balochistan and the fringes of Siraiki) Shah Abdul Lateef Bhittai; Sachal; Sami; spiritual treatise of Sain G. M. Syed; Shiekh Ayaz; Ustad Bhukhari; Ashu Lal; and Sufi saints.

Important question is that when cloned Dolly gets rebirth, how the genetically since can deny the philosophy and notion of liberation and rebirth?

Hazrat Mohammad (Holy Prophet – PBUH) and his blood lineage including Hazrat Ali (A. S.) were offspring of Hazrat Ibrahim A. S. (Abraham). *Durud,* a hymn, which ritually in Islam has to be chanted in association with prayers and otherwise, is acknowledged with the offspring of Hazrat Ibrahim having role for forwarding the massage of God through his religions. This also includes those human mediums that are not Prophetic, since the institution of Prophethood ended with the last Prophet Mohammad.

He, the Supreme Being, has sent the books through the Prophets, and also sent the massage based on

75

responsibility after the end of Prophethood. He, also has left the last holy book for the faithful in Islam, and the institution of *Ejtehad*, a similar medium of guideline for the faithful, and has infinite and diversified medium to keep on guiding humanity. No doubt, He is God of all generations, genders, eras, epoch, and periods, and of the existence in the universe.

Khudi (self), a Persian word which basically is a category and expression, is rooted in the word *Khuda* (God). This is where God and Person become one in a very much common expression and perception. God himself or herself? The very much mentioning of God is a limit of human in its very much linguistic expression and social realities of thinking in terms of gender. Human have not encompassed these dictates of their social evolution based on power influence of man on the rest genders inclusive of contemporary transgender aspects, which is a little beyond patriarchy. Therefore, the expression of *Khuda* and *Khudi* or Self (expression of God in the self) is beyond the limits of gender in terms of human, because when God and Person becomes one in Godly or Personally perspectives / aspects, the real state of existence becomes unfolded, and if blended with the all

76

connotations of social and spiritual expressions, the point comes where difference between theology, theosophy, Sufism and secularism cease to exist. Therefore, *Zaat* (Self) is a combined form of God and his connotations (*Safaat*). When, the connotations of God are separated from *Zaat* (self) they become *Safaat* characteristics in humanly terms. Linguistically, word Person or Personal are a mirage of human to see the things beyond the barriers of gender, society and in term of the planet. It is a linguistic connectivity with the universe, and vice versa. If Dr. Allama Iqbal's poetry is seen in this perspective, "*Khudi ko karbuland itna, khuda khud bandey se poochey, bata teri raza kiya he*" (Elevate your Self enough, that God may consider approval of person's own vision). Linguistically word Personality in the above perspectives, if seen with reference to Dr. Iqbal's '*Khudl* (Self) one can reach the separation of Self from God, where Dr. Iqbal proves to be a little tilted towards *Shuhudism* – an approach that detach God from person in the vision towards social affairs. That can be said appropriately whilst Dr. Iqbal, when wrote 'Gorakh Dhandha' while having *Hujat* -- a Self's contact with the Absolute Self -- with God, he was a little tilted towards *Wahdatul Wujud* – the Sufi-existentialism.

The diverse approaches in South Asia, have though manifestations in the politics, and the state expressions, however Sindhi Sufi Existentialist worldview spread across Sindh, Balochistan and Siraiki, has really been offering the path to our contemporary civilization, in terms of contemporary global civilization, by connecting the missing links of legacy in the urbanization of Indus civilization, through the medium of Sindhi Sufi world view based on Sindh journey from Veda through Bhagwat Gita, Bible, Kuran, and the message by Shah Abdul Lateef Bhittai, Sachal, and Sami. Indus civilization no doubt met with Yellow river civilization in Far East. It was Britain that created a new nation by human engineering in the history through blending Indusians with aboriginal Indonesians, which is now Indonesia. Suikarno Putri, which means Daughter of Suikarno,in a few languages of Indus civilization, is leader of Indonesia. It connects, colonial Delhi of Britain undivided India with Dili of Britain Indonesia. Sindhi have legitimate concerns and connectivity with democratic movements spread from Sindh to Indonesia. Karachi thanks Kathmandu, the Nepali people, for observing two days *Bandh* (shutter-down strike) against the judicial murder of Zulfikar Ali Bhutto. Karachi, the capital of Sindh culturally can be

78

called Sindhi-Baloch. For Sindh, like Nepal, Kathmandu means a market of wood.

Sain Nawab Kher Bux Muri, in himself was a unity between Sindh and Balochistan, like Nawab Akbar Khan Bugti, Saradar Attaullah Khan Mengal, and Sardar Mehmood Khan Achakzai, and like Nawab Raisani. He also was a unity among the people spread across the borders of Sindh and Balochistan in Afghanistan, Iran and in other countries.

It required to be expressed that when Moen Jo Daro met with Europe through Minor Asia or Phoenicia in terms of shedding culture through trade, Sindh and Sindhu are the real foundations of globalism, if not globalization, and of the contemporary civilization. Let us once have a glance at Rig Veda, and Holy Indus, and its capital in Sindh-Balochistan, and Siraki of today, to really meet the challenges of twentieth century we face in twenty-first century, and the development of the upcoming decades. Let the paganism and barbarianism of our own times, should not dictate out collective narrative and the decision making in the polity, interdependency and contemporary global civilization. Sain G. M. Syyed, said Sindh offers unity between and among diversity of religions. His Holiness Pope visited prisons in 2015 to see Muslim prisoners and left landmark impacts on world society. It was, in certain perspective, beginning of contemporary civilizations with reference to a new era. His Holiness initiatives for world peace; and with reference to salvation of humanity are milestone.

Sindh toady offers a global unity and connectivity between and among the diversity in the cultures, and in the making of our own contemporary human civilization.

80

6

CULTURALLY GLOBALISED

Neither languages, nor nations are pure. We together are inter-woven. This is the second foundation for the contemporary globalization. Anglicans are colonized in North America, Asia, Africa, Australia, and Europe. Spanish, French, Portuguese-Dutch are colonized in South America, North America, Africa, and Asia; linguistic Slav connectivity East Europe and Asia, Indo-European linguistic connectivity of Asia, Europe, North and South America, and Africa; Sindhi, linguistically and ethnically are merged in Europe, Asia, and Africa. Our historical merger is in Europe, especially in Eastern Europe, Italy, Greece, France, and Germany by Sinti (Sindhi) people. They are also called Roma people, because when Sindhi migrated to Europe, they first stayed in Rome centuries ago. They also stayed in Middle East in Kingdom of Saudi Arabia, Kurdistan in

Turkey, Iraq, Iran, Armenia, Syria and Jordon; in Eurasia particularly in Russia; and in Far-East. This Sindhi migration belongs to the era when Sindh, Balochistan, and Siraiki southern Punjab of today were Sindh – a country. Sindhi migration in modern age of human history was in Africa, and some above mentioned parts of Asia. A few Sindhi villages and settlements are in Bangladesh; most of these are centuries old and submerged there. Sindhi are submerged in Central Asian countries, Iran and Afghanistan. Arian colonized in Sindh of above mentioned era, northern and central India, and later on in Europe particularly Germany and Austria.

82

Sindhi, Persian and English have remained official languages of Sindh; this is the linguistic aspect of globalization. Sindhi and English are official language of Sindh today, along with English.

Iran means Arian land or nation. The political seat of Arians historically has remained Kabul and ethnic Gajar people of Iran. Anglo-Sexans of central Europe especially Germany and adjoining areas, invaded England, caused ouster of Englanders towards island of Ireland, which later on become Irish people. Germanic tribes migrated to Roman Empire as laborer, and according to Arnold J. B. Toynbee, the Germanic tribes destroyed the Roman Empire, which he mentions as 'external proletariat'.

Migrations in human history have important contours. The slave trade from African towards Europe and northern America was an in volunteer migration of Negroes there; and in Middle East, however the volunteer migration of African in Sindh of above mentioned era and later on, submergence of Arabs and Hebrews (Jews) in Sindh, and in the northern, central, southeastern and southwestern India of today; Arabs in Spain, and eastern Europe especially the Bosnia through invasions; submergence of Mongols in northeastern and central Afghanistan, northern Punjab in Pakistan, northern India and Iraq; Punjabis of Pakistan and India, Sindhi and Rajasthani in Indonesia, and Cambodia are the facts of history. Likewise, Tamil, Tibetan, and Bhutani had historical and recent submergence with Sri Lanka, India and Nepal. Ethnic Mongols and slightest submergence of Koreans is also there in China. China, unlike other civilizations and cultures, has historically remained isolated with reference to ethnic, linguistic and cultural globalization. Great Wall of China is the militaristic expression of it. The slightest submergence of Korean in India; Nepalis, Tibetan and Burmese (Myanmar) as well as south Indian slightest submergence in today's Sindh together with ethnic merger of all nations within and beyond nation-state 'nation' perspective contemporarily are the foundation of linguistic, sub-ethnic and cultural globalization across the world, combined with the communication revolution. Communication revolution is a contribution of USA in terms of invention of Internet and computer, and Russia inclusive of previous USSR states for space technology.

Sindh contributed in urbanization, urban planning inclusive of waste management, inventing digit 'Zero', wheal and weaving of cotton and silk to the human civilization; Euphrates and Mesopotamia (Iraq) contributed laws and constitution; Egypt contributed in mathematics and architecture. Maya civilization of South America contributed calendars, and Chinese Yellow River civilization contributed paper for writing and gun powder for firework. Iran although not a civilization, contributed whine to the world. Sindhi-Baloch fishermen of Karachi, in later era, contributed subsea swimming that can be called subsea journey and is well documented in the poetry of Shah Abdul Lateef Bhittai in his male Hero *Moriro*. His another Hero is Rai Diach. Rest of the themes of his poetry and philosophy is based on heroines. Rumi (Sufi saint, and poet philosopher) of Turkey is connected with Bhittai of Sindh through Iran, and Khusro of Turkey, who did poetry in Urdu is connected with Nizamuddin Aullia (saint) of India. The only difference is that Bhittai himself is Sufi, poet philosopher and Saint. In Sindh and Balochistan title of 'Saint' is virtually, philosophically and religiously equal to the order in Christianity.

Salafism has differences with the status of 'saint' from religious point of view in terms of Islamic jurisprudence. A major difference between Indian as well as Punjabis of Pakistan and Sindhi, Balochistani and Siraiki is that Indian and Punjabi Muslims do not allow women in the shrines of Sufi saints. However, Sufi Salafi, a Sindhi addition in *Salafism* schools of thought, has relatively more acceptability of Sufi saints with reference to religious aspect. Sufi Salafi term is coined by Shah Abdul Lateef Bhittai for that sub-school of thought. This, an addition of Sufi Salafi in *Salafism* by Sindh will help world to appropriately counter the challenge posed by terrorism in the name of Islam. The international terrorist outfits belong to Salafi sect. Salafi are a tiny minority among Muslim. Maulana Asadullah Bhutto, pervious Amir (President) of Jama'at –e-Islami Pakistan – Sindh Chapter and Naib Amir (Vice President) Jama'at –e-Islami Pakistan is Sufi Salafi. Sindh and Balochistan feel pleasure that the lands have contributed such sons and daughters in the fold of various religion-cum-sect based political parties, who can really connect political, social and theological doctrines of the sect with the challenges of the contemporary world and civilization especially fighting terrorism claimed to be in the name of Islam out of which majority belongs the Salafism. It is auspicious that Jama'at Islami, Pakistan recognized Indus civilization by hoisting flag of Ajrak, the cultural icon of Indus civilization having capital in Moen Jo Daro, on *Minar-e-Pakistan*, the symbol of Pakistan. Sindh and Balochistan, beyond the diversity of political thoughts and actions, always welcome the acceptance of Indus civilization by any ideology, school of thought, religion, sect or social group.

Wars are fourth tier for the globalization and contemporary civilization. Iran and Sparta war was the first inter-continental war that was waged for one hundred years. Sindh sent its Elephant warriors as military support to Iran. Sindh, with Buddhist majority and Hindu rule, sent military in the Iran war against Arab rule based in Baghdad (Iraq). Mohammad bin Qasim did not wedged war on orders by Hajaj bin Yousif because of Islam, but it was in a bid to revenge Sindh support to Iran.

Emperor Ashoka, born in Patli Putar (Patna) in Bihar, India was Prince of Indus Kingdoms seated in previous Hazara Division of Khyber-Pakhtunkhuwa in Pakistan, which were submerged by him into united India that is called *Akhand Bharat*. "Spread of Buddhism" is contribution of Ashoka besides uniting Southasian nations into Empire.

Chankya, who was teacher of statecraft and politics at Taxila University, was teacher of Ashoka. Chanakya is claimed by South Indians as well as by Sindhi. His ethnicity is still unknown. Chanakya migrated to Punjab temporarily, after his father migrated to Patna of today. Ashoka was given tough fight by Orissa (Kalinga of that time) state of today's India.

Jengez (Changez) Khan, the Mongol, and his offspring invaded China, Afghanistan, Iraq, Central Asian Countries, Sindh, Balochistan, Punjab, and India. They caused devastations and war damages to three civilizations Yellow River, Indus, and Mesopotamia. Urdu language is the only contribution of Mongols, who became "Mogul in Afghanistan" after invading Kabul; later on they submerged in Afghanistan, like in Sindh, India and some parts of Central Asia. In Sindh, majority of submerged Moguls is called Mogul and Agra because they invaded Sindh as well as migrated from Afghanistan and India. Those who hailed from Agra in India mostly use word Agra in their *Zaat* and those who hailed from Afghanistan are called Moguls; however some of the offspring of 1947 refugees are also known as Mogul. They do not speak Sindhi.

Alexander invaded Nile Civilization in Africa (The land of Pharaoh – Egypt and Libya; Mesopotamia in Middle East; Iran; and Sindh that was consisting today's Sindh, Balochistan, Qandahar, and Siraiki districts of southern Punjab. Hundreds of years ago, Punjab was having border skirmishes / conflict with Sindh over Siraiki areas, which form Siraiki district in today's Pakistani Punjab, and Pashtun areas of today's Balochistan. Punjab, having capital between Taxila and Islamabad at that time, welcomed Alexander and become voluntarily joined Alexander's Army. Sindh appealed other subcontinent nations for support against Alexander, which got no response.

Arab-Kurd-Turk led Caliphates and Ottoman Empire, known as Fatimid while based in Egypt, was having Jew Prime Minister; however the invasions and wars, and indulgence in crusades, put the foundation of united Europe. Foundations of continental unity and politics in Europe are laid in the crusades. Meanwhile, Navy is the contribution by Emir Muawiya of Islamic Caliphate. Formalizing diplomacy is another contribution of Caliphates and Ottoman Empires.

Urdu language (Mogul Indian) as well as title words like Czar (Russian) and Cesar (Roman) and Qaiser (Iranian) are examples of the linguistic globalization of wars by Empires. The wars that were between and among the nations of continents have contributed in internationalization. Julius Cesar's invasion of Egypt and Czar's invasion of Central Asia, and war with Afghanistan and Finland introduced Eurasian culture in Central Asia. Nursing is an internationalization initiative of the First and Second Word Wars besides foundations of the League of Nations, which later on became later on United Nations. Sindh who took part in the Second World War was not taken aboard like other participants of the Second World War for the process of United Nations. World Bank and International Monitory Fund (IMF) is the result of the world wars. North Atlantic Treaty Alliance (NATO) is the beginning of globalization and of contemporary civilization; and ISAF is the military addition to the contemporary civilization.

Militarization across the globe has created gender parity and transgender legality. Sindh and Balochistan does not only desire the due shared in their own governance including with reference to security and sovereignty, but also envision an engendered security regime. In Pakistan, participation of women, eunuch and religious minorities in the armed forces and services is a deep concern from the point of view social justice.

Along with war sciences, the development in the field of art of war as well as militaristic science inventions is also part not only of globalization but also of the contemporary civilization. Multiculturalism began with early migrations, boosted by internationalization of wars, and war making, and collective use of space technology by Europeans and thereby joint initiatives by North America, Asia and Europe is the contemporary civilization and globalization. Many things that include art of negotiations, deterrence perceptions, peace-keeping by international community and United Nations, the UN's initiative to serve Bosnian Europeans, who are Muslim as well, by undertaking their governance and government, "globalization and internationalization of medicines" is result of globalization process and is part of contemporary civilization. Besides, the trend to collective and multi-disciplinary research in the field of medicines and later on in space technology at higher level added into creating contemporary civilization based on the primary foundations of multiculturalism, help creating interdependence, collective initiatives, global laws with reference to outer space and its use, as well as legal connectivity with Universe.

90

Languages across the continents are connected. This is the foundation of contemporary global culture, a post multi-cultural reality that has to come in full expression as yet. Sindhi is a sister language to Sanskrit. It is a language of Moen Jo Daro, the capital of Indus civilization. Sindh, Balochistan and Siraiki southern Punjab has remained one country Sindh for centuries. Indus civilization or Sindh civilization has a linguistic fabric connected with the languages spoken in Sindh, Balochistan, Siraiki southern Punjab, Punjabi northern Punjab, Khyber Pakhtunkhuwa in Pakistan; Indian states of Punjab, Rajasthan, Gujarat, Haryana, East Bengal and Tamil Nadu in India; Kashmir in Pakistan,

India and China; Bengal, Tamil Nadu in India; Bangladesh; Sri Lanka; Nepal; Iran and Afghanistan.

Indus civilization in India is described as *Kutch ki Tahzeeb* (The civilization of Kutch) with reference to Kutch. In centuries old history, Kutch was capital of Sindh in the period of Kind Dodo Soomro. The second Hero of Shah Abdul Lateef Bhittai, Rai Diach, the Iconic King of Sindh, having Capital in Kutch, is focused treatise in the poetry of Bhittai, and later on in the poetry of Sheikh Ayaz, a legendry poet of Sindh in twentieth century.

The vocabulary of Sindhi, Balochi languages, Siraiki, and Gujarati and Rajasthani languages are shared to greater extent. The vocabulary of Sindhi, Punjabi, Hindko of Khyber Pakhtunkhuwa and Kashmiri is shared to certain extent. Sindhi and Nepali share their vocabulary to certain extent. In fact some places in Nepal as are associated with Sindh and Indus like Sindhu Pal Chowk, historical and official name of an area in Nepal. Sindhi shares vocabulary with Pashto and Persian to limited extent. Sindhi also share vocabulary with Urdu because Urdu is the latest, last and the newest language from united India having seat in Sindh as well as in Uttar Pardesh (UP) and Delhi in India. Bihari and Sindhi have some cultural resemblance that is evident in Biharis of Tarai in Nepal and Biharis in India, and in Bangladesh also. However,

91

ethno-linguistic Bihari immigration and influx in Sindh is post 1970 phenomena. There are phonetic and vocabulary traces between Kurdish, Spanish and Sindhi.

Sindh always have remained in favour of peace with India and Afghanistan. Sheikh Ayaz wrote a poem during 1965 war between India and Pakistan, the crux of which is 'Irony of War' "*Hee Sanghram, Samhoon Ahey Narayan Shiyam, Hun Ja Muhinja Geet Bi Sagiya*" (Irony of War. My departed Sindhi brother Narayan Shiyam is now on the land of India. And, we together share the same songs). He was jailed in Sahiwal prisons, in Punjab because of this poem. Other Sindhi leaders and hundreds of activists were also jailed in Punjab between 1965 to 2010 due to democratic and political rights activism and movement. Rasool Bux Palejo, leader of Sindhi Awami Tahreek, Awami National Party and Awami Tahreek (now Qomi Awami Tahreek), spent years in Kot Lakhpat jail near Lahore. Leaders and activists of all political parties from Sindh and Balochistan have been jailed for the similar reasons from Zero hours of August 14, 1947 to March, 2017. Those who took part in the Second World War on behalf of Sindh were handed over to Pakistan by Britain as Prisoners of War. Daily Guardian, London published news that Raheem Hingoro, a warrior, sentenced to death by military court of colonial Britain was hanged in Sindh Prisons Hyderabad.

92

Sindh and Balochistan together have always professed peace across the history, excepting the war waged in self defense, and against offense, and only have supported war allies until 1943 -- Iran, Germany, Japan, Turkey and Russia. Sindh profess globally self-defence and shares its experience of non-violent deterrence through non-violent and peaceful actions that it has observed during its decades in Pakistan as federating provinces.

Due to mountainous topography, thin population and sparse settlements, and having larger geographical area if compared with the other provinces in Pakistan is waging war because to Balochistan there is no other mean and method of protest. Non-violent and peaceful deterrence is Sindh philosophy shared with Balochistan and Siraiki people. This, based on the historical political culture of the lands, especially during their decades in Pakistan, is an addition to the philosophy of non-violence, peace and interdependence, professed by M. K. Gandhi, who did demanded M. A. Jinnah a travel without visa to Pakistan. M. K. Gandhi once said that it is responsibility of Gujarati to undertake development in Sindh because Sindhi are teachers of Gujarati. Sindh is thankful to Gujarati youth that undertook reconstruction work after the earthquake in Sindh in

1900s. Gandhi Ji himself once said to prominent Sindhi leader Dr. Choithram, "I am (M. K. Gandhi) Sindhi.

Nelson Mandela was an apostle of human equality because of his path of reconciliation between ethnicities and culture through non-violent means that has not only been educated and professed by the African culture before the world wars but also by the Holy Scriptures. It is also professed by the world community and United Nations. It is therefore, thus, suggested and requested that United Nations acknowledgment of Nelson Mandela's great contribution to humanity by declaring birthday of Mandela as Day against Apartheid and Discrimination.

94

Sindh-Balochistan together professes non-war use of nuclear technology. It is also formally mentioned that Balochistan Assembly during the period of Chief Minister Akhtar Mengal adopted resolution against nuclear tests by Pakistan. Simultaneously, G. M. Syed, Zulfikar Ali Bhutto leadership of Pakistan People's Party, Murteza Bhutto, Rasool Bux Palejo, Shah Mohammad Shah, Mir Ghouse Bux Bizanjo, Mehmood Khan Achazai, and others from Sindh and Balochistan have always opposed war against Afghanistan. Sindh leadership has been expressing its displeasure over the manner Benazir Bhutto was forced to sign formal orders for strategic interventions with reference to

Afghanistan. Sindh condemns the act of concerned quarters in Pakistani security establishment for refusal to sitting Prime Minister Benazir Bhutto, a Sindhi, of visiting nuclear processing facility in Punjab, despite that fact that Pakistan nuclear technology was a result of Zulfikar Ali Bhuto's decision, diplomacy and leadership.

Sindh and Balochistan believe that cultural interdependence, subsided by political culture of democratic norms in terms of not only holding elections, but also the actual trickle down of democratic essence into the actions at the government level and in the all tiers of governance. Democracy essentially is the economic democracy without which only structural democratic skeletons may exist, the soul and body politic of social and state interaction for development, peace and prosperity is impossible. Until this is not attained across the nations, which together form global community, the real transformation of world into contemporary civilization based on even globalization would be impossible.

95

7

GOVERNMENTS OF SINDH AND BALOCHISTAN

Sindh and Balochistan have been on equal page on the issues like Kalabagh Dam, coordination for inter-provincial crime counter mechanism, water resources sharing, flood management coordination and other similar matters. Karachi and other parts of Sindh have historically like, today, remained home to Balochistan during the winters, meanwhile Quetta and other parts of Balochistan have remained home to Sindhi historically and contemporarily during the summers.

Sindh Assembly is an exception since 1930s concerning issues of the legislation. In recent years, Sindh Assembly has legislated on numerous matters and issues ranging from child protection to the religious minorities like Hindus, which in accordance with Sindh are participation of Sindh into contemporary civilization as people and as a federating province among the nations of the world. Sindh legislation before August 14, 1947 legislated over matters related to gender, protection of birds, and other similar affairs that are Sindh contribution to the world in the context of world startup on gender rights and the responsibility towards life and environment on the globe. Sindh Assembly has already passed resolution for the Sindh's own military-force around 1997-1998 for the security. Government of Sindh has also declared the festival of Holi as public holiday, which Sindhi Hindu joined by Sindhi Muslim celebrate together. Chandra Keshab Sena (West Bengal) and Diya Ram Gindul Mal (Sindh) together took initiative for the legislation against the tradition of *Sati* in Hinduism. The tradition of *Sati* was banned by colonial Britain India.

97

Balochistan Parliament in united India has history of discussions and resolutions as well as legislation. Balochistan Assembly after 1948 has passed resolutions regarding in-volunteer disappearances, and the nuclear tests by federal authorities of Pakistan. Government of Balochistan decisions concerning national resources, demands with reference to Guwader, discussions in the Assembly sessions and the resolution by Balochistan Assembly whose elections were uncontroversial until 1998 passed resolution with reference to Guwadar Port, against federal designs.

Unlike Balochistan, Sindh has province wide police. Sindh Police, like Sindh Postal Services, were established by colonial Britain as role model for rest for united India. Some actions by Sindh and Balochistan Police officers, like other police officers in South Asia, has remained matter of concern for the people; however Sindh Police role is worth mentioned for emerging democracies in the undeveloped and developing world. Inspector General – IG (Police Chief) of Sindh Police refused Pakistan Army for merging military cadres in Sindh Police during 1990s. Another IG Sindh Police Syed Kamal Shah on the orders of Prime Minister House went to Jinnah International Airport, Karachi along with Police Force to arrest Pakistan Army Chief General Pervez Musharaf. However, during military rule, he was questioned regarding his action. The same IG also instructed Sindh Police in Karachi and held press conference as well that police should not interfere in the privacy of couples in the public places, and announced taking action against violators of instruction if complained. He announced telephone numbers for such complaints on which immediate action was promised. In Balochistan, the complaints against the Police are lowest if compared with rest provinces in Pakistan.

People of Sindh, on the line of Sindh Government during 2012 – 2014, demand that non-Sindhi cadres and personnel in Sindh Police neither should not be outsourced, nor should be submerged. Besides IG Sindh Police decision to not merge military cadre in

Sindh Police was seconded by the political parties of Sindh.

Sindh Police in 2009 decided not to join Balochistan Police for temporary merger to undertake police operation in Balochistan against political dissenters. A similar decision in Pakistan by one Punjabi General during the discussion on military action in East Pakistan. The military action happened however that finally turned into War of 1971.

Sindh and Balochistan, although have remained concerned regarding existence of tiny number of indigenous Sindhi and Baloch judges in Sindh and Balochistan higher judiciary, the decisions and verdicts by Sindh High Court as well as Balochistan High Court on enforced disappeared persons are exemplary. The district courts and other subordinate judicial mechanism, in many complaints against Sindh and Balochistan Police have done justice. In fact, Judiciary is the first ever state-oriented structure which became globalized across the world. And, 'will' of the people is above all.

Sindh and Balochistan have expressed their desire to undertake further governance reforms in all aspects, especially with support of United Nations and international community. Sindh and Balochistan thanked United States of America, and other countries for training and other support for police; Japan for road construction from Karachi to Quetta, RCD Highway; Iran for being first country dispatching humanitarian aid to Sindh during floods; and Sindh and Balochistan also thanked United Nations, Europe, North America, Asia and Australia for help supporting through various means in several areas of governance, legislation, infrastructure development, culture and tourism, especially education. Sindh and Balochistan desires to seek further support of United Nations and international community in various areas of interests, including participation in peacemaking, reforms particularly UN capacity building of Sindh and Balochistan Police concerning international laws and their practices, as well as rights regime.

100

8

SHARED POLITICAL AND CULTURAL RESOURCES

South Asia does not only share the natural resources and cultures, it also shares democracy, statecraft and secularism that is our collective contribution to humanity, sovereign states and the people.

In united India nearly two thousand years ago, the leading governance was *Maha Mat* (Prime Minister) which if translated, in Sindhi literally would means 'the most wise leader'. We also practiced in our earlier form of governance during the era of Kingdoms was essentially is shared by the Greek philosophy. South Asia has a legacy of *Maha Mat*, the wise Prime Ministers that includes on our part of Zulfikar Ali Bhutto and Benazir Bhutto. Chanakya's doctrines on statecraft and politics are gospel for the statecraft across the world. Benazir Bhutto, twice Prime Minister of Pakistan, mentioning secularism of southern Pakistan (Sindh, Balochistan), said once that we can share our experience of secularism with India. Prime Minister Zulfikar Ali Bhutto was mediatory between USA and China in 1970s for their alliance. Mao Zedong and Chu en Lai led China tilted towards USA when Zulfikar Ali Bhutto arranged an undeclared two-day visit of US President to China, in which Chinese and USA agreed on principle matters with each others.

Rashtray Suwym Sughatan (RSS) is the oldest political cultural organization in of volunteers in South Asia rooted in the theology and philosophy of Hinduism. It was founded in Sialkot city of Punjab, and its first unit after foundation was opened up in Nawabshah city of Sindh in united India. RSS does not participate in the elections. Apart from its political ideology, RSS is oldest political forum of South Asia that still exists with mammoth membership if compared with another similar organization Hindu Maha Shabha (HMS), which is older than RSS. HMS opposed the separation of Sindh from Bombay Presidency, is having a photograph of Sardar Sikandar Hayat Khan in its headquarters.

Molana Obaidullah Sindhi, a born Punjabi Sikh voluntarily chose to become Sindhi and Muslim, and added 'Sindhi' his title. Molana Obaidullah Sindhi was the Minister of Home Affairs of Government of India in Exile based in Kabul, Afghanistan lead by Subhash Chandra Bose. Sindh Sagar Party today is the continuation of Molana Obaidullah Sindhi's Ideology. Its interpretations of Islamic Jurisprudence are the guideline for the participation of Muslim in the contemporary global civilization. Molana Obaidullah Sindhi in his letter to Indian National Congress (INC) leader Jawaharlal Nehru he suggested that the name of INC should be changed into Indian International Congress because there are so many nations in united India.

Molana Obaidullah Sindhi was among the first who chose Sindh as their motherland, proved to be true some of Sindh. He proved to be one of the leaders of Sindh and of the Subcontinent. Some Scots as well as Englander Brits, Tibetans along with Chinese, Canadians, American, Iranians, Afghani, Africans, Iraqi, Turkish, Syrian, Saudis, Central Asians, and others chose Sindh as their land and are buried in districts of Karachi, Badin, Mirpurkhas, Hyderabad, Naushehro Feroz, and other districts of Sindh. Sindh and Balochistan are proud on these sons all of who played important role for Sindh, including waging wars and becoming the commanders in Sindh Army of the history. Simultaneously, Balochistan will always remember on equal footings the sons of soil who fought for the rights of Balochistan by being non-Balochistani. It is pride of Balochistan that Dutch, Afghani, Iranians, Central Asians, African, Iraqi, and others who chose Balochistan as their motherland, and have graves in Balochistan from the period of 1800s to 1980s.

Sindh had saint Mian Mir Sindhi, who born and brought up in Sewhan city, where Rig Veda was written on banks of Indus. Mian Mir Sindhi, a Sufi Muslim Sindhi, was invited by Sikh Masters to inaugurate Golden Temple, the holiest place for Sikhism. Majority of Sikh are Punjabi, and comes Sindhi, Rajasthani, and Pashtun. Guru Nanik Sahib meditated in Sadhu Bela, Sukkur, Sindh for long time before spreading the massage of Sikhism. Therefore Punjabi, Sindhi, Rajasthani and Pushtun are exclusively legitimate if they have any concerns about Sikhism, especially Punjabi in case if Sikh is of ethnic Punjabi origin also.

A verse of God in Rig Veda, the first Holy Scripture is also in Holy Kuran the last Holy Scripture – *Surai Ikhlas*. God, the Absolute Being, has introduced his Self in the first and the last book that He is beyond Time and Space, which is also expressed in a Sufi centre in Balochistan, called La *Hoot La Makan* (Beyond the time and space).

Zulfikar Ali Bhutto like a few statesmen, similar to Chanakya, was a 'thin line' between Yin Yan. The only examples of such in leadership in the contemporary times are Clinton and Blair who profess politics of

104

middle path; Markel of Germany; Putin in revival of Russia; and Shinzo Abe of Japan. Yin and Yan, is Korean-Chinese expression, which in Hegelian logic and Marxian philosophy is *Dialecticalism*. At least Hegel and Marx are agreed on Dialecticalism. Idealism and Materialism have their own stream. The debates of materialism and Idealism begins from Rig Veda, become thin line between Yin and Yan in Korea-China and contemporarily can be expressed Unity of Opposites in Dilectalism. Modern Sindh, in continuation of journey of human from Rig Veda to Islam and in philosophical terms to the Russell and Will Durant, and to the Sufi Sadiq Faqeer in Umerkot Sindh says, *"Allah Chadiyaun Aurahen, Parahen Paya, Bina Nam Supreen, Anjan ke Biya"* which means the Sufis united all characteristics (safat) of God / Absolute Being and turned his name God into Omnipresent unity behind the time and space, which is beyond time and space. In Rig Veda, this is called "Anaam".

Sindh apart from many other contributions specifically to Southasia, offered first among the indigenous political leadership to the united India after Emperor Ashoka in the form of Barrister Raees Ghulam Mohammad Bhurgri, a Muslim, who was not only among the founders of Indian National Congress (INC), the first Subcontinent political party, but also was earliest indigenous top leadership of INC. Jawahar

Lal Nehru and Mohammad Ali Jinnah joined leadership row of INC later on.

Gandhi Ji, while visiting Hyderabad, Sindh said Hyderabad is the most beautiful city of (undivided) India. Queen of Asia was the title used for Karachi by invader Charles Napier. Karachi had first Mayor Jamshed Naswanji Mehta. Jamshed was the maker of modern Karachi. In the city, G. M. Syed and Jamshed Nasarwanji Mehta incepted theosophical society in association with others, led by a Brit Theosophist founder. Sindh Theosophical Society had chapters in a few parts of Sindh including Hyderabad. Sindh Government is democratic enough that 'Sindh Freedom March' in 2009, 2012, and 2014 took place in Karachi, which were attended by millions of people, was not resisted by the authorities. The march had stage at Sindh Theosophical Society Headquarters near Tibet Centre in Karachi and was peopled around the mausoleum of Mohammad Ali Jinnah. Meanwhile, Sindh demanded protection and legislation for the cultural-religious freedom of the religious minorities by holding a march (2011), which began from Anne Besent Hall of Sindh Theosophical Society in Hyderabad participated by hundreds of participants. Government of Sindh, sensitive to the core issues of Sindh, did legislation and taken actions on some demands mentioned in the Memorandum. The slogan of protesters was Hindu, Muslim, Sikh, Christian, Sindhi

Nation, and Sindhi Nation. This blend of theology with Ideologies, theosophy, Sufism and secularism is enshrined in the culture of Sindh and Balochistan, a legacy of Indus civilization.

Sindhi is indigenously spoken in Sindh, Balochistan and to some extent in Siraiki South Punjab in Pakistan. It is also indigenously spoken in Rajasthan and Gujarat states of India and Sistan-Balochistan province of Iran. Balochi is spoken in Balochistan and Sindh in Pakistan. It is also spoken Helmand province of Afghanistan, and Sistan-Balochistan in Iran. Urdu in Pakistan has seat Sindh. Bihari, though latest migrants in Sindh, are well accommodated in the province. Persian in Pakistan has linguistic seat in Quetta, Balochistan, and historical seat in Sindh. In fact, Sindh was twice invaded because of being allied with Persian speaking Iran and Afghanistan. Mohammad Bin Qasim attacked and invaded Sindh because Sindh militarily supported Iran against Arab rulers. Britain invaded Sindh because it failed to invade Afghanistan. Britain also invaded Balochistan due to the same reasons.

Besides, Siraki is spoken in Siraki Southern Punjab, to certain extent in Sindh and in one district of Khyber Pakhtunkhuwa in Pakistan. It is also spoken in Bekanir region in Rajasthan state of India. Pashto is spoken in the Khyber Pakhtunkhuwa and Balochistan in Pakistan. It is also spoken in the several Pakistan bordering eastern Afghanistan provinces. Punjabi is spoken in central-northern Punjab in Pakistan. It is also spoken in Indian Punjab. Kashmiri is spoken in Kashmir – Pakistan, India and China. Gilgiti and Balti of Gilgit-Baltistan of Pakistan held Kashmir is spoken in Gilgit-Baltistan among the ethnic Bilavers.

108

9

MINGLING OF OCEANS

Rig Veda was written on the banks of river Indus near 109 Kirthar foothills. Word Sindh, Sindhu, Sindh Mahasagar and Sapat Sindhu are the names of Indus. Word 'Sapat Sindhu' mean the area of river Indus where seven other rivers of Indus river system finally submerge with it. This area falls in Sindh and Siraiki southeren Punjab. Rig Veda was written at the banks of river Indus near Sehwan at the foothills of scenic Bhagotorho. Sewhan city, the seat of a peculiar current of eastern-Indus Sindhi Muslim Sufism, has connectivity with Khyber Pakhtunkhuwa, Afghanistan and historical parts of Tibet in China. An old name of Sewhan city is Sevistan, mean Shiv Asthan, a land of Shiva. Nomenclature Sehawan, even today, is a combination of Siv and wahan(Sev-han -- Sehwan) which means Shiva's place. Prime Minister Birbal of Akbar's India was from Sewhan. Emperor Akbar's mother, Hamida Begum, was from Seeta village of district Dadu. Akbar himself got birth in Umerkot city of Sindh. Meanwhile, Mian Mir Sindhi, from Sehwan, inaugurated Golden Temple of Sikhism in Amritsar in Indian Punjab.

A 2000 years old Temple of Hinduism, the oldest surviving temple of Hinduism is in Nangarparkar town at the foothills of majestic Karoonjhar. Nangarparkar shares a smaller part in Indian mythology of earliest age. Sardaro in Nangarparkar is pilgrimage of Hinduism, and Gori Temples are the pilgrimage of Jainism in Mithi district near Nangarparkar. A *Tirthankar* (Prophet) of Jainism, one amongst last three before Lord Mahavir, was born and / or lived in Nangarparkar. Southern Sindh was Jain. Most of Sindhi Shia in southern Sindh use word 'Angaas' for Shia flag. Angas is the name of Jain Holy Scripture. Buddh surname is still exceptionally found in Sindh, especially on the both sides of Indus River in Khairpur Mirs district. Hinglaj Mata, near Hingol River in Balochistan is a Hindu pilgrimage in Balochistan. The great Sufi pilgrimage of Sindh-Balochistan is near Sindh-Balochistan borders is *La Hut La Makan* (No time, No space) – an existentialist Sufi pilgrimage that combines Islam with Veda, which is claimed to be beyond time and space. Until 1980s, most of Sindhi performed Haj in Lunwari Sharif in Badin district of Sindh, and Baloch are still performing Haj in Balochistan. They did not and do not go to Saudi Arabia for that matter. Haj performance in Sindh was banned in 1980 by General Ziaul Haq's military regime. Meanwhile, the Zikri Baloch of southern Balochistan performs prayers on the beat of music.

A research by Tel Aviv University of Israel mentions that Radhan Jews, a Jew tribe of merchants, use to migrate towards the direction of South Asia. They developed their settlements with the name of Radhan on the banks of rivers. The first Radhan was developed on the banks of Euphrates River in Iraq. Another Jew tribe, Gilel is submerged in South Asia, which is called Goel and Gilaal. Thus, the Goels and to certain extent Gilal's of Sindh and India are probably, Jews in their origin. Radhan is there near the bank of River Indus. It is one of the nearest towns to the historical Moen Jo Daro. Meanwhile, some in Dayaa communities in Sindh are offspring of Greeks that accompanied Alexander the Great.

111

Indus after Panjnad in Siraiki southern Punjab becomes a vast river, a Sagar (sea, literally). After Panjnad where five rivers of Punjab mingle with Indus, it was and can be called Sagar. In contemporary Siraiki poetry, the Indus is called, like historically, Sindh Sagar (Sea-like River Indus). We Sindhi call it Sindhu, the sea, and attribute it as Sindh Mahasagar, because it merges with Indian Ocean through Arabian.

Ashu Lal Faqeer, a contemporary legend in Siraiki poetry, wrote *"Sindh Sagar Naal Hamesha"* (with sea-like Indus, forever!). Earlier, the icon of modern Sindhi poetry blended with folk wisdom and diction, Ustad Bukhari, in his poem "Tareekh Mahasagar" (History of oceanic Indus) says:

I am the drop of oceanic Indus history,

Had a moon like flight in the clouds,

Around the globe,

In each corner and the continent,

Has just submerged with the soil of Sindh!

Shah Abdul Lateef Bhittai wrote the Vedic expression, *"Pachna, Khaaman, Pajraan"*. Similar expression was also given by iconic Hassan Dars, in contemporary Sindhi poetry, *"Aj bi muhinjedard men so dam aahey, Jan ta tunhijeychelhjo ko khamaahey"*. *Pachan* is a primary form of meditation (Jog / Tapasiya), in which one becomes like a hot iron, ready to take curve according to the touch of the perfect master, which is mentioned as *Dum* in above lines of Hassan; *Khaman*, becoming egoless, is the elementary of meditation, which is mentioned as *Khum* by Hassan; and *Pajran*, the third and higher state of meditation that requires a painful and deep process, is called *Dard* by Hassan. Hassan's lines clearly tell that Sindhi of today are the same hot iron, as they were in the Vedic era.

In Vedic perspective, this is the process of transcending from soul (Aatma), to saturated soul (Maha Aatma) for the oneness with Absolute Being (Param Aatma). This requires a threefold process of meditation, which is appropriately express by Shah Abdul Lateef Bhittai and contemporarily by Hassan Dars. Similarly, Sheikh Ayaz, the icon of modern Sindhi poetry, said in his copulate:

O Majesty, give a full-stop to time; and unwind it! *(Haan Sahib, waqtbeeharey chhad, hanin ji chaabi khaarey chhad).*This is the discourse about time and space, and no doubt has roots in Vedic Sindh.

Basically, Shah, Sachal and Sami are timothy of Vedic philosophy during the medieval periods. Shah Abdul Lateef Bhittai said that his philosophical hymns will be unfolded by SachalSarmast, and no doubt Sami, the last among the timothy, gave it a public glimpse with a brush stroke of Hinduism. Sachal Sarmast in one of his Siraiki poetry, *'Sufi hun Sarmastaa'* said, "this is a Sufi with a godly-shake, with whom (Shri) Ram himself shares smile". In his Urdu poem, *'Fana Baqa Men'* he says:

Be finite in the infinite,

And, submerge with the phenomenon of absolute beauty;

You are the absolute truth and reality,

You, just you have to become Being in yourself,

Thus, you, eventually, will become infinite by submerging with finite.

114

In brief, Shah Abdul Lateef is Hegelian expression of Vedic philosophy, theosophy and mysticism. No doubt, much before Hegel he did that. Sachal Sarmast is the Sufi-existentialist expression, and Sami is deeply rooted in the *Sanaatan* manifestation of Vedic philosophy.

115

10
CHOSEN LAND

Sindh is chosen land, together with Balochistan. The contributions of Sindh are Rig Veda and Moen Jo Daro. Sindh is honored by Jesus Christ according to a preacher of the Church of Canada that he was buried, with the Ajrak linen, a Sindhi block print used for all cultural happenings, also used for burial by Sindhi, Baloch and Siraki lands since over two thousand years.

While giving option to Yazid, the Arab Muslim King who killed family of Holy Prophet, Imam Husain, the grandson of Holy Prophet PBUH told Yazid that given him passage so that he may get settled in Sindh. Sindh was under Hindu rule and was a Buddhist majority when he chose to stay in Sindh. Holy Prophet PBUH is quoted as saying *"Hussain Mini, Wa Ana Min All Hussain"* (Holy Prophet expressed that he shares his features with Hussain, and Hussain shares feature of mine.) Like God in a verse of Holy Kuran said "Al Insan Siri, Wa Ana Sirahu" (Human shares my features, I share the feature of human).

God chose sacrifice among the Religions of Abraham (Hazrat Ibrahim A. S.) however, received the sacrifice by Jesus and Hussain -- both lineage of Abraham.

Sindh, thus, extends its experience of thousands of years-long journey of Indus civilization with the world for shaping contemporary civilization of our own generations and for the generations that have yet to come.

Powers can become past. The virtue of being superpower never. Sindh, inclusive of Balochistan, economically led this world for 1000 years between 5000 BC. USA, UK, France, Russia, China, Germany, India, Australia, South Africa, Japan and Brazil are the powers of our times. They the real and virtual vetoes power in the international community as well as centers of contemporary civilizations and economies. They are superpower. Sindhi were. Since Balochistan and Siraiki Southern Punjab of today was part of Sindh of that time, therefore they share virtue of being economies, civilization and urban development. Sindhi and Baloch, let us say, are the superpower of the past. No doubt, Indus sites are there in Gujarat and Rajasthan as well!

117

After the destruction of Moen Jo Daro, linguistic Brahvis of Balochistan today took to the mountains and Kurds migrated to the land is known as Kurdistan. In 1 century BC, according to the established history of Kurd people in Turkey, Iraq, Iran and Armenia, Kurd people migrated there. There are Kurds today in Bolan area of Balochistan, their tribal remnants like Chandiyas in Larkana and Dadu district exist.

118

11
INDUS DESCRIBES ISLAM

Sindh and Balochistan respect all civilizations and are part of contemporary one. The journey of religions that began with the kingdom of humanity, transformed into Kingdom of God in Christianity after Jews salvation by Moses. Jesus Christ said he will get rebirth on the occasion of the Day of Judgment. In Shia Islam, arrival of Akhir ul Zaman (the leader of last time for the world) is awaited. Day of Judgment is a shortest moment through which God will end the human world with the music, which would be an end to history with the end of human globe. According to the folk wisdom in Sindh, God housed soul in the human through music. According to the particle Physics, when Atom was further analyzed, anti-electrons, anti-neutrons and anti-protons were found. And, when these minor most elements were further analyzed, Quarks were found. Quarks are music according to Physics.

Dayaram Gidu Mal was an authority not only on Hinduism, Judaism, Christianity and Islam but also was authority on English, Hebrew, Arabic and Persian. A Sindhi Hindu Judge in the undivided Indian judiciary, Daya Ram Gidumal, resolved an issue with reference to Islamic jurisprudence, when two Muslim conflicting sects of India were not reaching an agreement with reference to the interpretation of Islamic jurisprudence in the matter. Both approached him. After proceedings, he issued decree, both religious parties accepted.

There are so many matters in Islam, which does not require *Ejtahad*. Only true and appropriate interpretation with reference to the contemporary realities of the verses of Koran would be the contemporary connectivity of Muslims with the Islamic Jurisprudence. Some matters no doubt, require *Ejtehad* in any way.

There are fallacies about Islamic jurisprudence. The true version of Islamic jurisprudence in Islam is:

1. There is no formally determined method of *Namaz* / Prayer in the Holy Koran.

2. *Tauhid*, oneness of God, is the first part of *Kalma'a-e-Tayyeba*, which means there is no god except Allah. The declaration of Mohammad (Peace Be Upon Him –

PBUH) as prophet is not part of *Tauhid*, it is the second part of Kalma, which is declaration of one's faith in the Prophet.

3. *Durud-e-Ibrahimi* (The Hymn of Abraham) is chanted / recited during and after performing *Namaz* (Prayers). Hymn of Abraham is for the offspring of Abraham (Hazrat Ibrahim A.S.). Holy Prophet Mohammad PBUH was offspring of Abraham. His daughter Fatima (A.S.) and his cousin Ali (A.S.) and others in his blood relations are also offspring of Abraham. Therefore, *Durud* – the hymn of Abraham is for the Prophets and Dietary in the lineage of Prophet Mohammad PBUH, and on those amongst non-prophets, who carry message of God through their works, research or inventions. Word *Allaih'a Salam* (A.S.) can be used for those, at least, who are eligible for Durud and / or Durud-e-Ibrahimi (The Hymn of Abraham).

4. *Surah-e-Ikhlas* is sent by God in his first scripture, Rig Veda according to Maulana Zakir Naik. It is also part of his last scripture Holy Kuran.

5. Muslims have to believe in all the books that are sent by God. Holy Bible mentions that Shri Ram is a

121

prophet. Muslims are bound to believe him as prophet of God.

6. Marriage between the *Ahl-e-Kitab* (people / persons following holly books) is allowed in Islam. There is no definition for *Ahl-e-Kitab* in Islam. Simply, it is meant that the individuals who have believed a code of living determined by God, through a holly book, can marry with each other. Followers to begin with the first Holy Scripture of Holly Rig Veda and ending at the followers of Holly Kuran, inclusive of Holly Bible can marry with each other.

7. Mohammad PBUH was son of Abdullah. Abdullah literally means the man created by God. If Holly prophet was the first who declared existence of Allah (God) in Arabs, then whose *Abd* (creation) was his father Abdullah? It means concept of Allah was already there in Arabia. Was this in Arabia through Christianity or Judaism? And, no doubt offspring of Abrahams (Hazratbrahim A.S.) were either Jews or Christians before Islam.

8. Consented sex is allowed in all Islamic orthodoxies – Hanfiyah, Shafa'i, Hambali and Maliki. This only requires two persons' consent and two witnesses. If witnesses unavailable, trees, stars and moon can

become witness according Islamic jurisprudence. Simultaneously, paid sex is allowed in case of emergencies and wars, according of Hadith, as well as jurisprudence. Besides, there are at least seventeen sorts of marriages as well as marriage deeds in Islam.

9. Islam gives the fundamental lesson of secularism, in which it terms religion a personal affair. Please refer to the Kuran verse, "*Lakum deenkum, wali-ye din.*"

10. Islam is to greater extent is jurisprudence of Moses (Hazrat Musa A.S.).

11. God in Holly Kuran says humans are created on my features; I am similar to human features. Please refer to the verse, "Al Insan siri, wa ana sir-a hu". At the same time, God in Holy Koran says, Oh human, I will be chanting about you, if you are destined to chant about me. God says in Holy Koran "labourer is beloved of God" (*Al-kasib habib-ul-aah*).

Muslims today do not practice *Ejtehad* in most of the cases. Pakistani scholars have not attended any practice of *Ejtehad* as yet in last seventy years.

12. Holy Prophet (PBUH) said that He is a Home of Wisdom. Ali is the door. How one can know in

accordance with His above quoted words about Koran, Islam, and Jurisprudence (Sharia) without going through Ali A.S.

In that perspective, *Nahaj-ul-Balagha* (Climax of Wisdom) the Book of discourses by Hazrat Ali are necessary for understanding and interoperating Kuran, Hadith, Sharia and Sunnah. Can any Imam of Fiqah (Interpolator of Islamic Jurisprudence – Sharia) can be more authentic if compared with the Wisdom of Ali A.S. in the Climax of Wisdom? Besides, the *Jafferia* interpretations of Islamic Jurisprudence is in accordence with Hanfiya orthodox. (Imam Abu Hanifa's *Maslik* – Orthodox). Jaffria interpretation is by Imam Jaffer Sadiq, great grandson of Holy Prophet of PBUH, is practiced by Shia; and the interpretations by Imam Ismail, great grandson of the Holy Prophet PBUH is practiced by Khuwaja Shia Ismaili.

13. *Farz* is an obligation in Islam. Rest is not. Even Sunnah (the life style and practices of Holy Prophet PBUH) is not mandatory.

14. *Hadith* – mostly quoted sayings and practices of Holy Prophet by others are contradictory. According to Muslim history, most of the sayings by Holy Prophet PBUH and the practices are documented by Abu

Huraia. Abdu Huraira became Muslim shortly before Holy Prophet's departure (death). There is an incident in which Bibi Aysha A.S. contradicted the narration of a saying by Holy Prophet when Abu Huraia shared. Abu Huraia did not buy her version. Therefore the only authenticity about the Islam is Holy Koran.

15. Consent of male and female for marriage is obligation in Islam. When a person is married without one's own consent, mostly on the parents will or wish that relation of intercourse is called *Zina*. While Rape is called Zina bil Jabr. This means, if un-consented by marrying parties, and without will, the act of intercourse is called Zina bil Jabr. One can marry without the will / wish of parents similar to what is legal through the Courts in Pakistan and other parts of the world.

16. There are more than seventeen kinds of marriage bonds according Islamic orthodox of Hanfiya, Shafai, Humbali, and Maliki Orthodox (*Maslik*). Besides, consented intercourse for an agreed period, if shared with at least two persons as witness of agreement, is part of Islamic Jurisprudence. In case of absence of witness, according to Jurisprudence, natural existence like trees, moon, and others can be made witnessed

before God. Consented / periodic intercourse and relation is allowed in the Islamic Republics as well as Muslim majority countries in Middle East, Iran, Malaysia, Indonesia, Egypt and many others.

17. Intercourse in lieu of money, according to Hadith, and Muslim history, is allowed in case of wars and emergencies. According to the narration, Holy Prophet PBUH was asked during a war that warring Asahaba were away from home (their wives), therefore they require having intercourse. Holy Prophet PBUH replied that they can have intercourse if female in the area have consented, and are paid appropriately. Paid intercourse is allowed in the Islamic Republics as well as Muslim majority countries in Middle East, Iran, Malaysia, Indonesia, Egypt and many others.

18. Liquor is not *Haraam* (forbidden). Haram is a Jurisprudence ban by the order of God in Islam. For a period not more than ten years, there was no verse from God on the use of intoxicants. Only when, *Asahaba* (those who saw Holy Prophet PBUH) performed Namaz inappropriately, a fundamental of Islam called Farz, the verse revealed that the Prayer cannot be performed while intoxicated. God did not say that do not use intoxicants. By doing so, he fulfilled

his words that he can forgive *Huqooq Allah* (obligations to God), but not *Huqqooq al Ibad* (obligations to the human). He preferred abstaining Prayer, not the intoxication. There is no particular verse that is an order by God for declaring intoxication Haram. The verses related to the matter of intoxication particularly of liquor only mention the damages to health due to use of it, and there is a verse that abstaining performance of Nimaz (Prayer) in intoxication. Therefore, there is no punishment in the world and after Day of Judgment for intoxication. God himself has offered liquor in Heavens according to Holy Kuran. Before this, the Prophets have also been using and offering the liquor, like according to New Testament (*Injeel Muqadas*) Jesus Christ invited his students for liquor.

19. Holy Prophet was not only for man, he was for nature as well. It is assumed that the status of *Harram* for pork was in a bid to save species of pig / bore. Although bore is *Haram* in Islam, the specie of pig / bore is extinct in Arabia.

20. Islam's unacknowledged contribution is a framework of rights regime for women. God, according to Koran will call everyone on the Day of

127

Judgment with the names of their mothers. How God would have called persons for the Judgment with the name of fathers, if Jesus got birth without father? Besides, he is responsible to contain everyone's privacy. If a consented intercourse happens and a female conceives, and in case the father of the baby is socially unknown, how than God disclose the privacy (secrecy) of the persons, both female and male. In Europe and Northern America, identity of parents is mandatory with the mother's name.

21. *Ejtehad* is an institution through which scholars and representatives of various groups will deliberate on the issues of the world and take decision on it collectively according to that times requirement. *Ejtehad* is exceptionally used in Islam.

There is a controversy that in Koran whether the use of world 'seen' is for China or for Sindh. Indus was also called Abaseen.

Sindhi Muslim and Hindu, above ninety percent of Sindhi across the world believe together at least in two books – Rig Veda and Shah Jo Risalo. Sindhi Muslim primarily follows Quran in the religious practices, and

Hindu follows Bhagwat Gita and some other scriptures in religious practices. Since Rig Veda is the first Holly Scripture, its currents are strongly available in Holly Scriptures of Hindus, Jews, Christians, Buddhists, Jains and Muslims. And, Sindhi of all sorts follow the spirituality of Shah Jo Risalo, the poetry (Hymns) of Shah Abdul Latif Bhittai. Shah Jo Risalo is further expressed by Sachal Sarmast and Sami. Sindhi are also Christians, Zoroastrians and Sikhs.

12
WORLD POLITY AND OCEANIC INDUS

On the banks of Indus, in southern Punjab, Siraiki poetry '*Sindh Sagar Naal Hamesha*' (with oceanic Indus, forever!) is a massage for flowing with the wave of Indus. The wave of Indus is submergence with contemporary civilization of globalization and connectivity with the universe in all of forms. Sindh and Balochistan acknowledge that led by USA, Russia, Europe, and India we together are connecting with the universe. It is the contribution of USA in terms of country, with the collective scientific contribution that it protects the physical sovereignty of the globe by taking measures against steroids. This is the beginning of an important aspect of the contemporary global civilization. The wave of Indus is an important part of it.

This is an age of *continentalism*, according to Asif Baladi, in his discourse two decades ago. Asif Baladi is an intellectual and previous Secretary General of Jeay Sindh Qomi Mahaz (JSQM).

JSQM a political party that leads the largest popular peaceful social movement for teretorial freedom and sovereignty in Asia, and if combined together with Sindh based political parties, the movement of Sindh is the largest amongst the peaceful and non-violent movement in the World. Since militant Sindh Liberation Army (SLA) has not has caused killing of human and animal according the news reports, therefore freedom movement in Sindh is peaceful and non-violent. JSQM also popularly demanded freedom of Sindh and Balochistan both in front of some millions people from activities and mobilization in and around Sindh Freedom March from 2009 to 2014 according to the news reports. In fact it is the second largest political party in Sindh and third largest people mobilization party in Pakistan. The liberation movement of Balochistan is violent; because due to high altitude mountains and very small population, people of Balochistan cannot observer peaceful protest.

131

In the age of contemporary global civilization, where world slowly is pacing towards observing an epoch, for a new "leap of faith" based of calculated madness for our own contemporary civilization. Brexits of their own kind are simmering everywhere due to nations transition from older order to the new global order. Nations take decision in today's realities and in accordance with their own contemporary interests. At this juncture, the forums like Common Wealth of pervious British dominions and colonies, and Common Wealth of Independent States of previous Soviet Union federating states also needs to have pace with this development. It is suggested that a Common Wealth of Indian Subcontinent States should be established.

A federation is agency that provides collectivity in terms of sovereignty, security and interests from territorial and people's perspective. If a federal mechanism fails this of its political, philosophical, and foundational responsibility, and it does not transform in bid to fulfill this responsibility, welcoming new sovereign countries with the 'will' of people would be the only way forward.

Sindh and Balochistan today are in Pakistan. Historically they have remained independent and sovereign countries for centuries since thousands of years. Sindhi and Baloch want to secede. They also participate in the political and parliamentary process in Pakistan, which is their sovereign and democratic right. A few millions in Sindh have protested in Karachi for freedom of Sindh during 2009, 20012 and 20014 as well as have caused and resulted into mobilization in Sindh. War for the freedom / secession of Balochistan is underway since at least a couple of decades. There are also political parties in Sindh and Balochistan (and

Khyber Pakhtunkhuwaa and Siraikis as well) that want provincial autonomy. In fact, Sindh and Balochistan require sovereign autonomies due to political and other reasons in Pakistan. Whether they will have sovereign autonomies within or beyond Pakistan? Time is the best judge.